PRAISE FOR
FIND YOUR HAPPY AT WORK

"Beverly Jones presents invaluable information to get past any obstacle at work and, at the same time, helps the reader be happier in life. The stories she shares allow the reader to feel a connection with those she has coached, and the strategies at the end of each chapter are game changers. Her thoughtful but direct approach to this topic is refreshing and much needed today."

—Joan Lynch, chief content and programming officer, WorkingNation

"Beverly Jones delivers on this book title's promise. *Find Your Happy at Work* is filled with practical, bite-sized tips to help each of us move past our work doldrums and find more meaning and happiness in our day."

—Scott Shute, head of mindfulness and compassion at LinkedIn and author of *The Full Body Yes*

"*Find Your Happy at Work* is for anyone who has found themselves stuck in a job—bored, insecure, or simply consumed by a nagging feeling of being undervalued and overlooked. Beverly Jones provides a superb and insightful playbook of how to take control of your challenges and truly engage in your work, be inspired, productive, and, yes, happy."

—Kerry Hannon, author of *Great Pajama Jobs, Never Too Old to Get Rich, Great Jobs for Everyone 50+,* and *Love Your Job*

"Beverly Jones is filled with so much knowledge about how to approach your own career, and she is adept at delivering advice in a way that is easily consumable and relatable. Navigating a career today is no easy task, but Beverly has helped me and many others find clarity and purpose through it all."

—Ryan Lytle, social media strategy leader at Adobe

"Reading a career tip chapter by Bev Jones is like having a wise counselor with a gently authoritative voice sitting next to you offering the best advice that money can buy and that you can realistically follow. A pure pleasure."

—Ira Chaleff, author of *Intelligent Disobedience*

"Work is, after all, work. But Beverly Jones tells you how to make it fun and rewarding. And along the way, you'll find ideas on how to get more out of your leisure time, too."

—John Maxwell Hamilton,
Hopkins P. Breazeale Professor of Journalism,
LSU Manship School of Mass Communication

"Happiness is not only possible, happiness is here with Beverly E. Jones's new book, *Find Your Happy at Work*! An inspiring and authentic series of proven strategies to affect positive change in your workplace and with yourself. Extremely helpful and practical, meeting today's complex challenges as America goes back to the office."

—Earl Johnson, author, *Finding Comfort During Hard Times*

FIND YOUR HAPPY AT WORK

50 WAYS to Get Unstuck, Move Past Boredom, and Discover Fulfillment

BEVERLY E. JONES

CAREER PRESS

This edition first published in 2021 by Career Press, an imprint of
Red Wheel/Weiser, LLC
With offices at:
65 Parker Street, Suite 7
Newburyport, MA 01950
www.careerpress.com
www.redwheelweiser.com

ISBN: 978-1-63265-186-0
Library of Congress Cataloging-in-Publication Data available upon
request.

Cover design by Kathryn Sky-Peck
Interior illustrations © Karen Deans
Interior by Timm Bryson, em em design, LLC
Typeset in Adobe Garamond Pro

Printed in the United States of America
IBI
10 9 8 7 6 5 4 3 2 1

For Andy. Teamwork!

CONTENTS

LIST OF ILLUSTRATIONS

ACKNOWLEDGMENTS

As always, I'm grateful to my journalist husband, Andy Alexander. Once again, he has been a tactful and supportive editor.

It is also handy to have sisters who are professors. Neuroscientist Helen Burroughs went through my chapters with care, checking for scientific accuracy. Communications expert Libby Vick tried to bring my language and assumptions up to date. Thank you both for reading through my draft and setting me straight.

Thanks also to Kerry Hannon and Susan P. Joyce for providing expert chapters. Kerry is a high-profile career and finance author, journalist, and speaker. Susan is a superb career writer, and her site, *Job-Hunt.org*, is *the* place to go when you're hunting your next gig.

I love the illustrations drawn by multitalented artist and author Karen Deans. Thank you for taking on this small project.

Thanks much to Tom Hodson, Adam Rich, and the wonderful team at Ohio University's WOUB Public Media. Hosting the *Jazzed About Work* podcast these last few years has been a joy and a vital part of my continuing education. Thanks also to our wonderful and talented guests, including those—like Tom—who show up in this book.

Among many other supportive Ohio University friends, I thank Dean Mark Weinberg for many years of partnership with the Voinovich School of Leadership and Public Service. Congratulations for the wonderful growth of the Voinovich

Academy for Excellence in Public Service. Our work together has inspired topics in this book.

Once again I thank my excellent agent Cindy Zigman of Second City Publishing Services. You make this process so much easier, and I appreciate your willingness to stick with me.

I want to thank my clients and mentees, many of whom have encouraged my writing since long before my first book. All good relationships are reciprocal, and you are my teachers.

Thank you also social media friends from around the world. During the long process of writing this book, I was encouraged by frequent posts and comments about my first book, *Think Like an Entrepreneur, Act Like a CEO.* Twitter friends have been particularly lively, as you may see if you follow me @beverlyejones.

Finally, thank you, Career Press, for keeping me in the family. Let's have some fun with this book.

INTRODUCTION

Some people always seem excited about their work. Sure, they go through crises like everyone else, but they bounce right back, energetically tackling their next challenges.

Sadly, these folks are a minority. Long-term studies show that roughly two-thirds of American workers often feel unhappy in their work lives. Despite occasional moments of job satisfaction, they frequently are bogged down in boredom, loneliness, fear, or resentment.

Are you in this second group? Feeling stressed? Frustrated? Professionally adrift? Wondering how to feel good about work again?

You're not alone. Most of us feel stuck or uncertain at times.

Research by the Gallup organization over many years suggests that only about a third of American employees typically are "engaged" in their jobs. These people are "involved in, enthusiastic about and committed to their work and workplace."

When you're "engaged," you feel positive about what you do. Not only are you happy, but also you're likely to be helping move your organization—and yourself—forward. You're on a path to success.

The story is different if you're among the 53 percent Gallup describes as not engaged. You don't feel so great. You try to complete your required tasks, but finding the energy to go the extra mile or break new ground is hard.

If you're among the 13 percent that Gallup describes as "actively disengaged," you're in deeper trouble. You are not happy.

By acting out your unhappiness on the job, you may be making things worse.

If you're not enjoying work, it's time to make some changes. For one thing, when you are happier, you'll be more productive. Optimistic and motivated workers achieve more than their negative, disgruntled peers.

Career success is only one thing at stake here. You devote a huge portion of your life to your occupation. Your relationship to work impacts everything—your health, your family life, even the way you see the world.

This book can help you become happier in your work. As an executive coach, I've worked with thousands of professionals and know positive change is possible, even in the dark times. Transforming your relationship with work may be easier than you think.

Even if you're feeling trapped, remember that you *own your career. You can change your work life if you want to. The starting point is with you, today.*

The book first looks at the basics of career happiness. This is not an academic treatise, but please know everything I talk about is rooted in behavioral science. *Research says that every one of us has the power to adjust our attitude, enhance our skills and intelligence, reinvent the ways we approach life, and even change how our brain operates.*

With this book we explore how the choices you make can shift your work experience. Beyond the fundamentals of professional fulfillment, we focus on how you're more likely to remain enthused and successful at work when you pay attention to your health and the activities that make life satisfying for you.

We also discuss techniques for handling some of the trials and distractions that might get in the way of a good day at work. Many chapters examine specific challenges and offer practical solutions so you can find greater enjoyment, meaning, and achievement on the job.

I've shaped the book like I might frame an ongoing discussion with a coaching client. As you read the chapters from start to finish, we return to some issues and go deeper as we move along. At the end of each chapter are suggested exercises or key takeaways.

In my mind I see you using this as a workbook, and I imagine you making notations in your e-book or scribbling notes in the margins of paper pages.

Because you're busy, I've also made each chapter a standalone discussion of a specific topic. You can jump around the chapters, picking those that address issues you may find most troublesome on any particular day.

Throughout the book are true stories about real people. In some cases they're lessons from the experiences of my clients. When I mention a person only by a first name, I am referring to a client or mentee whose identity I've masked to protect the confidentiality.

Often suggestions for a rewarding career are illustrated through the words of guests on my podcast about careers, *Jazzed About Work* (you can hear it on *NPR.org*). An asterisk appears next to the name of each podcast guest, and the appendix lists the dates of relevant podcast episodes.

Much of the research and most examples are drawn from the United States, but the principles are universal. My first book, *Think Like an Entrepreneur, Act Like a CEO*, brings me feedback from around the world, and I am struck by how the same points seem to resonate with readers, whether they are in Africa, the Middle East, or Australia.

I became intrigued with many of the book's topics during my earlier career as a lawyer and later as a corporate executive.

Since then, as a career coach, I've explored these concepts and strategies with countless clients.

While no job is permanent, you probably do* not *have to change jobs to find more joy in your work. You can shift your attitude and choose simple steps to get unstuck, beat back boredom, create deeper meaning in each day, and once again be enthusiastic about your career.

Chapter 1

You Can Make Work
Feel More Like Play

Sometimes play seems like the kind of activity that can make us happy, as opposed to work, which can feel like a drag.

True, play is fun, and it seems we have evolved to enjoy it. For human children and other young mammals, it's a vital learning opportunity, a chance to acquire social and other skills that allow us to thrive later in life. But when we reflect on our lives, the contrast between work and play isn't that stark.

The difference between work and play is something I discussed with my client Mia, who manages eight multimedia journalists within the communications operation of a large, successful organization.

When we first spoke, Mia said she probably shouldn't be complaining about her career. Producing media projects was what she'd always wanted, and she felt lucky to have some job security. Yet Mia was unhappy with her job and wanted to take action.

One issue was the relentless deadlines, but her discontent stemmed from more than the pressure to get things done. Mia saw herself as working harder and better than her boss, colleagues, and direct reports. However, she believed she didn't get a fair share of respect. She fretted constantly about perceived slights, missed promotions, and other ways her career felt stymied.

Soon, however, Mia's life changed significantly. First, her father had a heart attack, and within weeks her husband was diagnosed with cancer. After years of disciplining herself to focus mostly on career success, Mia quickly redirected much of her energy to taking care of her family.

As Mia navigated through a few difficult months, her attitude toward her career shifted. With much of her attention elsewhere, she stopped obsessing about past slights and stalled upward mobility.

Mia relaxed her insistence on perfection and gradually abandoned her need to control every detail. Doing so enabled her to see other ways of getting things done. She became better at delegating tasks, coaching staffers, and rolling with the punches when things didn't go as expected. In a matter of months she became a stronger, more optimistic leader, with a new appreciation for her supportive team.

As the health of her dad and husband improved, Mia found herself once again excited about going to work. Her mindset had changed, so instead of resuming her control-freak ways, she concentrated on empowering her team. She also had fun by working directly on creative projects.

Mia said that her work now felt more like play. Nothing had changed in her job description. But for her, everything had changed.

THE SAME ACTIVITIES MAY FEEL EITHER LIKE WORK OR PLAY

In our final coaching session, Mia and I revisited the topic of play versus work. *The distinction is not that work requires more effort than play.* When you watch kids playing baseball or grown-ups playing tennis, they're clearly trying hard. When Mia turned again to hands-on creative work, she worked with a new intensity, loving every minute of it.

In fact, making an effort is essential to both the gratification of meaningful work and the fun of engaging play. It takes effort to learn something new, build a deeper skill, or finish any kind of rewarding project. Exerting effort in any activity is part of what makes us feel alive.

Part of the difference is that work is more tied to a *duty.* You're obligated to someone else, like your boss or client. In contrast, pure play is something you *elect* to do because you enjoy it. Here's where it gets interesting: an activity required by your occupation can feel more like play when you choose *how* to do it.

In Mia's case, she'd become consumed by anger and insecurity, and trapped by her need to control things beyond her reach. Exhausted by micromanaging, she lost the ability to experiment and innovate.

Mia's mindset shifted dramatically when her concern for her family disrupted her insistence on control at the office. She stopped worrying about getting credit and rethought her narrow view of how leaders should act. As Mia encouraged team members to pursue tasks in their own way, they became happier. And so did she.

I wasn't surprised to see Mia feel happier, because her experience is consistent with the research. ***Science says some measure of autonomy—and the opportunity to be inventive, work in your own way, and draw on your strengths—is a basic human need.*** Finding a more positive way to engage in your work, like Mia did, will make you a happier person.

TO MAKE WORK FEEL MORE LIKE PLAY, BE AWARE OF YOUR CHOICES

Throughout this book I talk about ways to modify your situation and find more satisfaction in your work. If you don't want to wait, you can take a step toward happiness *right now* by choosing to do something in a way that's outside your normal pattern.

I understand you may feel stuck. Some of that comes from your habits, your routine way of looking at things, and perhaps a negative voice in your head. The challenge can be to get out of your own way.

You probably have far more chances to make decisions on the job than you typically notice. If you make even one new choice, you might feel a little better.

Looking for a bit of independence doesn't mean you want to avoid responsibility or let down your boss. Rebellion is not required. Exercising autonomy might mean approaching assignments with a more positive attitude or a personal style that better aligns with your true values.

Even in a rigidly controlled environment—an airplane cockpit, a hospital operating room, a busy restaurant kitchen—you can select how to approach each task. As we explore in future chapters, you have endless opportunities to make slight shifts, like deepening your focus, changing your attitude, or listening more intently to other people.

EXERCISE:

When you consciously decide to try something new or change how you manage a familiar task, you cultivate a sense of accomplishment. Your new choice can lead to a quick feeling of success, and that will make work feel less like drudgery.

To make work feel a little more enjoyable, try these techniques:

1. **Say "thank you."** Feeling even a glimmer of gratitude can improve your day. So think about someone who has been helpful and express your appreciation. Whether you send a note or speak up in a meeting, the gesture will make you both feel better.

2. **Do it differently.** Even tasks you enjoy can become tedious with too much repetition. If a project feels dull, look for ways to change things. Whenever possible, expand your skill set and deepen your expertise.

3. **Quit whining.** Adjust your attitude by shifting your focus from things that bother you. Watch for your *urge* to complain, whether aloud or in your head. When you feel a complaint bubble up, shut it down before your words tumble out. Instead, say something positive, either aloud or to yourself.

4. **Eat a frog.** Does your mood plummet when you look at the tedious overdue tasks on your "to-do" list? Mark Twain said if you eat a live frog in the morning, nothing worse will happen to you the rest of the day. His advice would be to tackle a small but distasteful task *now* so you have it out of the way. The relief that comes from "eating a frog" can inspire a more cheerful outlook.

5. **Create a game.** Give yourself thirty minutes to rush through as many small tasks as you can manage. Don't dither about how to do something—just get it done. Then count the items you've completed—keeping track of accomplishments is satisfying and part of the fun.

Chapter 2

Feeling Upbeat Helps You Succeed

Coaching clients often sound apologetic when they talk about wanting to be happier at work. It's as though they think feeling good is unprofessional. But that's not true.

In this chapter I talk about what it means to be "happy." And I touch on a few of the reasons being happy is so important, including at work.

A simple definition of "happiness" is that you're feeling good. You're cheerful, you're enjoying life, and you hope your contentment can continue.

While people experience happiness in different ways, the positive emotions of happy people commonly are accompanied by a deeper sense of meaning and purpose. Long-term happiness often includes a sense of being connected with other people and a feeling of contribution to the greater good.

In contrast, when you're *un*happy, you feel miserable. Maybe you have a sense of isolation, or you're overwhelmed by stress and anxiety. Your mood is gloomy, which can sap your energy and drive people away.

Remember Mia from Chapter 1? In our initial conversation she worried that she'd have to choose between career success and her growing desire to be happier. That wasn't the case. For her, happiness and career accomplishment seemed to arrive hand in hand.

To spend time at home, Mia placed more trust in her team, and an unexpected consequence was that she had more fun at work. Then gradually, as a by-product of her new leadership style and more positive attitude, she and her team became more creative and better at meeting their goals.

Happiness and success are similar in that you can't pursue either directly. Each seems to emerge as a consequence of the way you manage yourself and your activities.

As with Mia, a chicken-and-egg loop often ties happiness with success. You try something new, and it works better than the old way. The accomplishment makes you feel more confident and relaxed, so you're in a great mood when you meet with a colleague. Soon the two of you create an even bigger plan, and you both enjoy the success.

Throughout the 20th century, industrial psychologists studied the relationship between positivity and productivity. Their work indicated that happy workers accomplish more than their unhappy peers. Upbeat people tend to be healthier, get along better with their colleagues, and are more likely to be strong leaders.

Until more recent advances in brain science, researchers continued to wonder: what comes first, the happiness or the success? Now the results are in, and positive emotions clearly are the starting point for career success.

In *The Happiness Advantage*, psychologist Shawn Achor explains that years ago we were taught that if you work hard, you would be successful. Now "new research in psychology and neuroscience shows that it works the other way around: We become more successful *when* we are happier and more positive."

Positive emotions—and the chemical changes they bring—alter the way our brain operates. For example, we make more neural connections, which allows us to solve more problems and become more innovative. Happiness also helps us be creative, partly because we're open-minded and better able to process new information.

I tell even my most goal-driven clients not to apologize for wanting to be happier. A more satisfying work life brings many benefits. When these professionals find ways to make the daily grind feel more like play, they set themselves up for career success.

You can do that too.

— KEY TAKEAWAY —

You don't need to choose between career success and feeling happy. If you commit to becoming more optimistic and create a work life that brings more enjoyment, your positive emotions will fuel your career success.

Three Keys to Finding Satisfaction at Work: Purpose, People, and Performance

You can't just flip a switch to make yourself feel more contented, but you *can* steadily, methodically cultivate happiness. In this chapter we lay more groundwork by examining three factors that are key to enjoying work. Future chapters explore many ways to nurture positive feelings, move past barriers, and develop a more optimistic view of your work and your life. I hope you try some of the end-of-chapter exercises and experiment with the key takeaways. As you build a more satisfying work life, you may learn to better support colleagues and grow as a leader.

That was the case with Roberto, a brilliant economist who recently had become manager of a small branch within a government agency. Roberto supports his agency's mission and felt honored to step into leadership. He knew his new job brought challenges because the branch had a record of low performance. So he prepared thoroughly and arrived at his new office with several good ideas for improving work processes.

I first spoke with Roberto after he'd been in his new job for about six weeks. He was starting to feel discouraged. He had convened several group meetings to introduce ways to make his unit more successful but hadn't been able to generate any enthusiasm. He worried that his team members were hopelessly disengaged and reluctant to take direction from a new leader.

In our first conversation, I asked questions that helped Roberto reconsider the best way to motivate his team members. After he vented about the group's apathy, we began to focus more specifically on each individual.

We talked about how most people want to do well at work, but not everybody is motivated in the same way. Roberto had chosen team meetings as the place to generate excitement about making the branch more effective. After we talked, he shifted gears.

He decided to develop a specific strategy for each of his seven direct reports. He wanted to get to know each person, help each feel more positive about the job, and gradually improve productivity.

To help Roberto explore an attitude improvement plan for each staffer, I introduced him to a simple three-point framework I often use when coaching clients around issues related to happiness at work. I call it the "Engagement Triangle."

When you're fully engaged at work, you feel physically and emotionally energized, you're mentally focused, and your activities are in keeping with your values. Work that promotes full engagement isn't always fun—think of challenging jobs like emergency room nurse, firefighter, or foreign correspondent. But being engaged in something meaningful can bring you great satisfaction, even on a tough day.

Modern research and centuries of wisdom suggest you're more likely to engage—and thus are happier at work—if you remain aware of three basic factors: your sense of purpose, the human relationships associated with your job, and the most satisfying and productive ways to approach your tasks.

If you're a leader, analyzing the needs and strengths of each team member in terms of the Triangle can help you motivate the group. Whether we're considering our own situation or trying to understand others, most of us focus more heavily on one or two

ENGAGEMENT TRIANGLE

The three points of the Engagement Triangle are vital to your happiness at work.

areas and may neglect the third. So a checklist can be useful in promoting a thorough discussion.

When I ask a client like Roberto to "do the Triangle," we talk through a work situation by exploring this detailed outline:

ENGAGEMENT TRIANGLE

1. **Purpose:** *It's easier to love your job if you're working for something that matters more than just a paycheck.*
   - Your purpose is something bigger than your everyday self and is likely to include an impact on other people.
   - Your work may have meaning because you support the vision of your organization. Many strong organizations frequently mention their core principles. Mark Dagostino and a group of Zappos.com employees* wrote *The Power of WOW*, which opens with the

Zappos company purpose: "To inspire the world by showing it's possible to simultaneously deliver happiness to customers, employees, community, vendors, and shareholders in a long-term, sustainable way."

- Your immediate team's values can be motivating even when they're unstated. People tend to share a sense of purpose in groups where everyone's work is appreciated and the result is superior service or a solid product.

- Your pride in providing an excellent product or service can make every day feel meaningful. Your personal mission at work can encompass the values that guide your broader life, like kindness and integrity.

- Even a tedious job can feel rewarding if you have a good reason for working so hard, like supporting your family or preparing for your future career.

2. **People:** *Your job can feel more satisfying because of your colleagues, your broader circle of clients and professional contacts, and other people you encounter in the course of your career.*

- When you feel connected with others and believe you're making a contribution, your outlook on life is more positive.

- Having friends at work is a key to high performance and job satisfaction. People with close friends at work are likely to be happier and better at engaging customers.

- Studies say we accomplish more when co-workers show each other respect, gratitude, trust, and integrity.

- In *The Culture Code*, author Daniel Coyle says highly successful groups tend to develop a culture that feels much like a family. In strong teams people have a

sense of belonging, communicate constantly, and feel safe around one another.
- Especially if you work by yourself or in an unfriendly environment, you might need to broaden your network and cultivate additional relationships. You can feel connected even when you're working alone.

3. **Performance:** *You're more likely to love your job if you invest effort in your tasks, build expertise and remain interested in your work, and exercise some autonomy.*
   - Time passes quickly when you have challenging tasks and opportunities to build something. It helps to be able to use your strengths, move toward clear goals, and get regular feedback.
   - When work feels dull, you can stimulate fresh energy by learning something new. The sense of achievement that comes from acquiring a different skill or deeper knowledge can spark an upward spiral.
   - Workers who decide how to get a job done are happier and more productive than their micromanaged peers. If you're feeling micromanaged, focus on the decisions that you can control, and make repetitive tasks more interesting by finding ways to improve the process.
   - Your tasks may feel more exciting if they support other people, contribute to the shared vision, or broaden your role within a group.
   - You can find considerable satisfaction by simply doing your job well and meeting your obligations. You'll enjoy it even more if you keep finding ways to improve your work.

The arrows that surround the Triangle in the illustration are a reminder that purpose, people, and performance are connected. When you have a sense of purpose, you remain aware of how your activity impacts other people. When you approach your work with diligence, your approach is shaped by your values. And an awareness of other people can bring more meaning and satisfaction to all that you do.

The Engagement Triangle can help you plan your good days and feel better on your bad days.

Roberto used the Triangle to observe and think more deeply about each person on his team. It helped him build relationships, be more strategic while assigning projects, and better support individual success strategies.

For example, Roberto's senior economist seemed hopelessly bored, so he looked for new projects she might find interesting. After he helped her snag an opportunity to write an article for a leading journal, she began to exhibit fresh energy and a more positive attitude.

Before Roberto started using the Triangle to shape conversations with team members, I suggested he get a feel for the three points by thinking about what makes *him* feel optimistic and interested at work. He elected to start each workday by quickly writing answers to these three questions:

1. **Purpose:** What core value will I keep in mind during my work today?
2. **People:** Who will I remember to appreciate in the course of the workday?
3. **Performance:** What task will I perform with special attention?

The Triangle helped Roberto in two ways as he turned around his branch. It gave him a structure for thinking and talking about each staffer's strengths, challenges, and goals. More significantly, this basic outline helped him reflect on the things he cares most about in his career. As he reconnected with his own goals and values, Roberto began to relax, become a better listener, and communicate more successfully with his team.

EXERCISE:

To create your own version of the Engagement Triangle, at least once a day for a week pick one of these *P*s and write about what it means to you:

1. **Purpose:** List reasons why *your* work matters. This might mean anything from supporting your family to providing a critical public service.

2. **People:** Name folks you have come to know and appreciate through your job, including those affected by what you do. Or consider other types of professional relationships that might help you grow.

3. **Performance:** Describe how you have fun and enjoy a sense of accomplishment on your best days. Describe the kinds of service that your occupation allows you to offer others. Or identify areas where you want to build expertise.

Chapter 4

Transform Your Career with a Strong Purpose Statement

In Chapter 3 I described how career happiness may reflect the way you manage the three *P*s of the Engagement Triangle:

- *Purpose*, including your values and mission,
- *People*, both those at work and in your broader career, and
- *Performance*, providing satisfaction as you approach and complete tasks.

I've seen many variations on this simple three-P formula for loving your work. I thought about the endless possibilities one day as I sat in a salon chair, getting a haircut.

THIS HAIRSTYLIST HAS MASTERED A HAPPY-AT-WORK FORMULA

I schedule my cuts months in advance because Jason Holloway, my ponytailed hairstylist, has a full calendar and a long waiting list. Typically, Jason works at his salon four days a week and serves clients six to eight hours a day. Unlike others I've known, he never double-books, squeezing in a second client for a quick cut while ignoring his first one who is waiting for her color to take.

I love that when I reach Jason's chair, he's always ready and focused entirely on me and my hair. I know his small business has substantial overhead, and I suspect he could make more money if he were to put in more time or serve his clients at a faster pace.

I asked Jason if he thought about adding hours to his salon schedule or finding ways to fit more clients into each day. "No," he said, "if I'm just grinding it out, it shows in my work."

Jason started his career as a shampoo boy. Then he studied and worked his way up, moving from salons to corporate work. Eventually, he reached a high tier of the hair industry, crisscrossing the country for cosmetics giant L'Oréal to teach hairdressers the latest trends and techniques. He liked being a trainer, enjoyed learning the ropes within a major company, and was making more money than he had time to spend.

Jason, however, found the constant travel to be exhausting. He felt burned out and wanted to find "peace." So he decided to leave the big time, move about seventy miles from the Washington, DC, area to the small Virginia town of Culpeper, and create a career that supports the life he wants.

Now, with his own small salon, Jason is proud that clients book months ahead. Most important, he is happy and self-aware, and regularly thinks about the key values that frame his work life.

Here is how Jason describes the career formula that helps him remain joyful and productive:

1. **Start with the people.** Once he launched his business, Jason moved carefully to find compatible workers. He trained an apprentice, April Carter, and recruited two friends as part-time colleagues. Jason consciously builds real relationships with his clients, focusing on each one intently and looking forward to visiting with his regulars. He understands that having friends at work is incredibly important to job satisfaction.

2. **Build your skills.** Jason has developed strong technical skills and continues to study the latest techniques for cutting and coloring. He loves not only doing hair but also finding ways to support each client's hopes and goals.

3. **Know your mission.** Jason regards hair as a kind of calling: a combination of art, science, and service to others. Every day he remains aware of the joy in understanding and nurturing his clients.

4. **Pursue additional career activities.** Jason is passionate about his salon but wants variety in his career. So he leaves time for producing and selling art, including photographs. He has a real estate license and also teaches yoga classes. By pursuing several career paths, Jason is always learning something new, which is key to enjoying work. And a strong sense of mission contributes to Jason's happiness.

A SUCCESSFUL HOTELIER FOUND HIS FORMULA YEARS AGO, IN AN INSTANT

About twenty-five miles from Jason's salon, in the tiny historic Virginia town of Washington, I met Klaus Peters*, who is driven by mission and seems to glow with love for his job.

Klaus is a distinguished gray-haired man with a slight German accent and beaming smile. Today his labor of love is running the Foster Harris House, a lovely B&B he purchased after suffering through a "boring" but short-lived retirement.

Before his mini-retirement, Klaus enjoyed a successful career in top American hotel chains. He was the resident manager of several premier hotels, including The Watergate and The Fairfax at Embassy Row, both in Washington, DC.

Klaus started his career in Europe, at the bottom, as a fourteen-year-old kitchen apprentice. His German father had lost everything during World War II, so in the late 1950s young Klaus helped support the family. After working his way up to serving, at age eighteen, he answered an ad to become a waiter at a Texas hotel.

In a LinkedIn post Klaus wrote that in those days in Europe, if you were a German at the low end of a hierarchy, you were treated like a nonentity. "In 1964, I arrived in Houston as a 'Nobody' server, at the Hotel America . . . making $3.50 a day plus tips," he said. "I had low self-esteem and thus became arrogant to cover up my insecurities. I don't believe that I was liked by too many people."

Then a miracle happened: Klaus was given the opportunity to serve dinner to the hotel manager, Earl Duffy. "Just imagine, Mr. Duffy greeted me by name and introduced me to his guests and his guests to me," Klaus said.

"WOW, this had never happened to me before. Mr. Duffy respected me and treated me like an equal. To him and his wife, I was a 'Somebody.' The way he made me feel totally changed my personality and the way I would treat subordinates in the future," he said.

Klaus's life was transformed by the sudden realization that you can shift another person's sense of self and behavior, by acknowledging them and treating them with respect. So Klaus adopted the mission: "Treat everybody like a Somebody." By the time he was twenty-six, guided by his mission statement, Klaus was managing a Florida resort and loving his thriving career.

SOME PEOPLE DEVOTE YEARS TO CRAFTING THEIR RULEBOOK

For Jason and especially Klaus, articulating a clear mission statement has been transformative. Other people do better by developing a more complex set of rules to guide their lives.

Shawn Askinosie* writes about his personal guidelines for living in his moving and insightful book, *Meaningful Work*. As a younger man, Shawn was a hard-charging criminal attorney who loved his demanding job. But he grew tired and realized that if he didn't change gears, the work would kill him. So he began thinking about his life goals and spent five years creating his new vocation.

Today Shawn is CEO of Askinosie Chocolate, a Springfield, Missouri, company that makes small-batch, direct-trade, artisanal chocolate. Bars are made from single-origin cocoa beans from Tanzania, Ecuador, and the Philippines.

The chocolate is delicious, but beyond that Askinosie cooks social responsibility into every bar. The company keeps open books and shares profits with the farmers who grow their beans. It goes beyond business relationships to partner with origin communities, creating programs like providing 2,600 free lunches for local school children.

In his book, Shawn talks openly about how he developed a detailed "Rule" of life. His Rule seeks balance as it sets out Shawn's daily behavior in four areas: prayer, study, recreation or enjoyment, and work. At the end he lays out his daily, weekly, monthly, and annual schedules, which is "where the rubber meets the road."

Shawn's Rule was developed through years of reflection and with guidance from a Trappist monk. *He says you don't need a monk to write a rule that can guide your life and vocation. The starting point is an explanation of why you want a rule in the first place.* From there you anchor it to your faith or to something else that's bigger than yourself.

Shawn recommends beginning with a statement of personal values and allowing your professional statement to emerge as you choose areas of your life that you want to balance.

EXERCISE:

Write a first draft of your professional mission statement. The format doesn't matter. You can describe your personal or professional vision, or a summary of your key values, in many different ways. Start with the three *P*s of the Engagement Triangle and answer these questions:

1. **Purpose:**
   - How does my profession help people or serve society?
   - What do I hope to accomplish?
   - In what do I excel?
   - What standards and values do I bring to my career?

2. **People:**
   - How do I treat other people?
   - How would I like to have other people describe me?
   - What values do I want to find in the places I work?
   - What are the relationships I value the most?

3. **Performance:**
   - How would I like to have others describe my work?
   - What accomplishments do I find most satisfying?
   - What should I be learning next?
   - What standards should I aim to meet with every task?

Chapter 5

Sometimes Crises Lead to Growth and Deeper Engagement

Personal and professional mission statements often evolve over time, but sometimes change starts dramatically, in a flash.

Journalist Mark Miller* discusses how this might happen in *Jolt: Stories of Trauma and Transformation.* His book features inspiring true stories about people who survived a traumatic life event, like the death of a child, and then somehow found a way to transform their lives and emerge stronger than ever.

During our *Jazzed About Work* podcast interview, Mark said he became interested in resilient people while he was researching "encore careers." These are late-life careers built around a social purpose, like helping sick children or supporting community journalism.

Mark noticed some people make an occupational shift and devote themselves to doing good only after "their sense of meaning is blown away" by a terrible event in their lives. He became intrigued by this type of career reinvention and found that psychologists describe this rebound from crisis as "post-traumatic growth," or "PTG."

In explaining the PTG syndrome, *Jolt* describes a married couple whose son died in the World Trade Center on 9/11. The husband and wife explored a variety of local organizations in hopes of dealing with their grief by helping others.

Nothing felt exactly right until they were inspired by a TV news story about mental health challenges in post-conflict societies in Africa. Mark said this story "grabbed them by the throat," and they started a nonprofit to establish mental health facilities for survivors of conflict.

Mark says it's not clear how some people are able to rebuild their lives after a life-changing shock while others struggle to bounce back, even from the smaller traumas that arise in everyday living. Often a successful transition involves feeling empathy for others, discovering a sense of gratitude, and cultivating an awareness of things that matter.

In *Flourish*, psychologist Martin Seligman says that modern research on resilience and PTG is consistent with ancient wisdom. Both philosophy and data suggest "personal transformation is characterized by renewed appreciation of being alive, enhanced personal strength, acting on new possibilities, improved relationships and spiritual deepening."

In future chapters we explore how Seligman and others have demonstrated that a hopeful, positive attitude is critical to personal transformation in any kind of situation. We look at ways to develop more positivity, even if you were born a pessimist.

— KEY TAKEAWAY —

Sometimes life brings terrible shocks and difficult times. If you focus on the future and don't give up, your grief or frustration can serve as the passage toward a rewarding new mission and satisfying life.

For many going through a life change, it can take a while for a fresh vision to emerge. Shawn Askinosie said it took him five years to move from his law career to the launch of his socially responsible chocolate business. Yet there can be meaning and a sense of achievement even during the early days of a new vocation.

Chapter 6

Journal Your Way to a Happier, More Productive Work Life

Notice that many of my end-of-chapter exercises ask you to write something.

The reason: Overwhelming evidence indicates you're more likely to master and integrate a new idea into your behavior if you write about it in your own words.

You'll get more from this book if you write about the topics discussed. Yet I resisted the urge to begin this book by suggesting that to be happier at work you should journal about it.

Why?

Because if you're already keeping a journal, you don't need me to tell you how helpful it can be.

If you don't keep a journal, it's probably not because the thought never crossed your mind. I know from years of working with clients that the habit of regularly journaling doesn't click with everyone. One reason is the challenge of squeezing out a few minutes from an already-overbooked schedule.

Aside from all the times I've watched clients struggle to keep their journals up to date, here's a confession: I absolutely believe in the amazing power of managing work and life by keeping a journal, yet I can't always do it.

I keep a system going for a while and remember why writing every day is so powerful. Then something shifts and my commitment fades. Sometimes that style of journaling just doesn't seem to fit anymore. Maybe I was just writing lists, but now I need more reflective prose.

I'm not going to lean on you to start journaling to get the most from this book. *But I want to suggest that if you've ever flirted with the idea of journaling as a way to bring change to your life, now is an excellent time to start. Here are some of the reasons journaling can help you be more engaged at work:*

1. **Writing boosts learning.** When you write about something, your brain processes information in a more thorough way than it does if you're simply reading or listening. As your brain sorts and arranges categories of information, your subconscious may slip into problem-solving mode, generating insights and memories.

2. *Handwriting* **boosts deep learning.** Studies say writing *by hand* can further enhance the learning process, partly because it requires more thought about each word you put on paper. Also, the complicated motion of your fingers stimulates your brain in ways that keying in words does not.

3. **It's healing.** "Expressive writing" is a technique where people write about their feelings, perhaps describing a health challenge or a difficult experience. In a typical study, participants might journal for fifteen to twenty minutes a day, for three or four days. Results vary, but research suggests that for many people this kind of exercise can help strengthen the immune system, lower blood pressure, support a quicker recovery from surgery, and reduce chronic pain.

4. **Journaling helps you address tough questions.** As a safe place, your journal is a venue for tackling questions that otherwise might keep you up at night. Keeping a journal allows you to examine your strengths and challenges, develop a more precise understanding of potential threats and possibilities, and trigger insights that otherwise might not reach your conscious mind.

5. **It can stimulate gratitude.** Cultivating an awareness of gratitude can make you happier. Our brains are wired so

that we can't feel anxious at the same time we're feeling thankful. Beyond that, grateful people are more likely to be empathetic and less likely to suffer from envy or resentment, and so they get along better with others. A powerful way to use your journal can be to keep a daily "gratitude list" of things and people you appreciate. The trick is to pause and *experience* a feeling of thankfulness as you write each item.

6. **You can reach goals more quickly.** Your journal is an important tool for getting things done. If you're working toward a goal, noting your progress can help you stay committed and on track. Your journal can help you articulate a precise goal, take steps toward achieving it, and record what you do each day.

— KEY TAKEAWAY —

Because journaling is such a powerful practice, it could transform your outlook, bring new clarity and creativity to your work, and make each day more satisfying.

There's no right or wrong way to journal, as long as you do it regularly. Some people like to jot notes throughout the day on their smartphones. Others love to sit in a quiet place and write in a beautifully bound book. If you want to try journaling, consider starting with the end-of-chapter writing exercises.

Chapter 7

Taking Care of Yourself Promotes Happiness

Finding fun and satisfaction in your career is possible even when things aren't going well in the rest of your life. For some people work serves as a refuge from discomfort, grief, or conflict at home.

But it's difficult to do your best work and harder to achieve happiness when you aren't in good shape physically, mentally, and emotionally. True happiness is rooted in every part of your being.

There's a constant interplay between your mind and body. Your thoughts and emotions reverberate throughout your physical self and influence the way your brain operates. So even a single positive step, like creating a gratitude list, has the potential to trigger a significant shift, bringing new awareness and helping you let go of stress and feel better.

The mind-body loop is just as active when you don't feel so good. It's tough to be cheerful when your body is tortured by signs of stress, your mind is hijacked by negative self-talk, or your life feels out of sync with your value system.

Cultivating happiness at work isn't just a matter of tweaking what you do on the job. Supporting career happiness includes being as healthy as possible in all spheres of your life: your mind, body, emotions, and spirituality. As you care for any aspect of your health, you will be nurturing the full scope of your well-being.

Definitions of *well-being* differ, sometimes depending on the professional expertise of the writer. The term suggests you are happy and engaged in life today and anticipating happiness tomorrow.

Psychologists might say that you have well-being when you accept yourself, enjoy positive relationships, have good mental health, and find meaning and satisfaction in your life. Economists say well-being also requires prosperity and productivity.

Others argue that a feeling of accomplishment is so important to mental health that a description of well-being must include a sense of achievement from meaningful work.

Tom Rath and Jim Harter, leading researchers at Gallup, suggest "career wellbeing" is a fifth realm—one that's essential to a thriving life. In *Wellbeing: The Five Essential Elements*, they say, "If you don't have the opportunity to regularly do something you enjoy—even if it's more of a passion or interest than something you get paid to do—the odds of your having wellbeing in other areas diminish rapidly."

— KEY TAKEAWAY —

Although well-being means different things to different people, there's widespread agreement that it's linked to workplace satisfaction and performance. It's hugely important to how you can live your life.

Chapter 8

Health and Happiness Goals Lead You to Well-Being

Chasing well-being in the midst of your busy career takes conscious effort. But many easy steps can move you in the right direction.

I've often discussed well-being with my friend Gayle Williams-Byers*, a municipal court judge in South Euclid, Ohio. Gayle worked for me years ago in Washington, first as a student intern and later as a lawyer. Even back then she was a powerful woman, determined to succeed in her career and give back to the inner-city Cleveland community where she grew up.

In the early days, I often spoke with Gayle about work/life balance and the importance of exercise and a healthy diet. She'd pay lip service to taking better care of herself, but she felt far too busy to alter her workaholic habits.

Much later, as co-chair of the Education Committee of the American Judges Association, Gayle saw how many of her colleagues were struggling emotionally. They were exhausted from the pressure of being responsible for people caught in difficult situations like domestic violence or mental illness.

Gayle says the tragic events judges deal with every day leave some of them suffering from "vicarious trauma." In a podcast interview she said the stress from dealing with difficult cases, day after day, pours into judges' personal lives and impacts their ability to do their best work.

4 REALMS OF WELL-BEING

The four realms of well-being illustrate the mind-body-spirit-emotion loop of health and happiness.

Now Gayle believes passionately that training for judges should go beyond "hard skills" and developments in the law to include strategies for promoting well-being. When teaching her colleagues, Judge Gayle's motto is "self-care is not selfish."

This image is a model Gayle and I used for a well-being workshop at a national conference of judges. It draws from a number of well-established sources to illustrate how four areas of well-being are interconnected.

Following are some of the factors associated with each of the four realms of a flourishing life:

1. **Body**
   - Exercise and fitness
   - Sleep and rest
   - Nutrition

- Stress and tension
- Energy and vitality
- Movement
- Comfort

2. Spirit

- Purpose and mission
- Where you find meaning
- Values and morals
- A sense of connection
- Goals that go beyond self
- Courage and determination
- Fairness and justice
- Transcendence and spiritual health

3. Heart

- Feelings and emotional health
- Love
- Relationships
- Self-worth and acceptance
- Calmness and coping
- Optimism and resilience
- Gratitude, compassion, and kindness
- Stress management
- Joy

4. Mind

- Acuity and mental health
- Thought and self-talk
- Beliefs and values
- Perceptions
- Focus and attention
- Mindfulness and awareness
- Curiosity and learning
- Brain health

TO ADDRESS WELL-BEING,
START WHERE IT'S EASY

The four realms of well-being are so tightly tied together that you can intervene at any point. Typically, the best way to approach an issue impacting your well-being is to begin with whatever activity seems easiest and most accessible.

As Gayle began to encourage other judges to take better care of themselves, she examined her own life. She acknowledged that the challenge of making tough decisions every day, while remaining unbiased, had become intensely stressful. She saw how the pressure was hurting others around her, causing her family to suffer.

For Gayle, improving well-being included nurturing her most important relationships. It began with small changes, like staying up later at night, talking deeply with her husband, Greg. Then, gradually, her first efforts blossomed into bigger shifts.

Gayle said her favorite well-being initiative is the "ninety-day rule in our marriage. It requires that every ninety days we take some kind of trip or vacation, just the two of us." The outing could last a day or a week, but it always turns out to be meaningful.

Beyond her ninety-day rule, Gayle says she continues to explore other steps toward a healthier life. For example, she finds that regular exercise helps her be her best self. She says walking every day not only exercises her muscles but also helps release the emotions that—as a judge managing difficult cases—she is not permitted to discuss with other people.

One of Gayle's favorite techniques is to build greater awareness by using a quick, four-step process known as the "STOP tool."

I first read about this mindfulness technique in Timothy Gallwey's 2009 book, *The Inner Game of Stress.* Here's Gallwey's version:

1. **Step back.** Notice what's happening and put distance between yourself and the situation.
2. **Think.** Take a few deep breaths; then consider the truth
   about what's going on, as well as your feelings, priorities,
   and options.
3. **Organize thoughts.** Come up with an action plan.
4. **Proceed.** Move forward with your work, with new clarity
   and understanding.

— KEY TAKEAWAY —

There are many avenues for building well-being. You can
begin wherever it feels easy and right for you. You may
see progress after even a few tiny steps.

For example, say you're feeling stressed. You might like
to deal with stress by talking about emotions, which
could mean coffee with friends.

Or you might reduce stress by getting fit and
enjoying better physical health. To start an
upward spiral by caring for your body, your
new regimen might include changing your sleep
habits, eating better, or getting more exercise.

Chapter 9

Move Forward with the Sugar Grain Process

Because you're reading this book, I'm guessing you don't feel like you're flourishing at work or maybe in other parts of your life. Or perhaps things are okay, but you know they could be even better.

It's normal to crave change. Some of the most rewarding moments in life come when you're trying to make improvements. In this chapter we talk about a powerful technique for creating the change you want. First, though, some background.

HOW I LEARNED TO CREATE
BIG CHANGE BY TAKING TINY STEPS

As a teenager, I stumbled into an understanding of the power of gradual change. It all began because my siblings and I learned from our New Zealand–born parents to drink plenty of hot tea. For us kids, a cup of tea meant several spoonfuls of sugar.

When I was about fourteen, I worried that I'd gain weight. I knew I should probably give up sugar, but the prospect of drinking the tea I loved without the added sweetness seemed just too hard.

One day inspiration struck. As I held up a heaping teaspoon of sugar, it occurred to me that I could pinch away a few sugar grains without noticing a taste difference. In the following days I removed a few more. Over the course of a year, I gradually cut the amount of sugar in each cup until I was enjoying unsweetened tea.

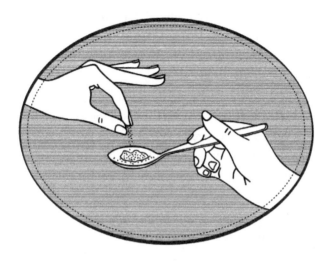

The "Sugar Grain Process" suggests how to create change one grain at a time.

Capturing the power of incremental change has helped me manage my life ever since.

The sugar grain technique came in handy in my early twenties, when I stumbled into a wonderful opportunity at Ohio University. Because of my activism in support of equal educational opportunity, I landed a job as assistant to the university president for affirmative action and issues related to women. My job included creating programs to help women students and faculty members move into jobs that previously had been closed to them.

It now seems difficult to believe, but before passage of Title IX of the Education Amendments of 1972, many academic areas were closed to women. Universities explicitly barred them from admission to professional programs like law, engineering, and medicine. The rationale was that graduate education was wasted on women because they'd inevitably quit work to have babies.

Not only did women have limited access to grad school, but other university policies gave preferential treatment to men. For example, per anti-nepotism rules, if both members of a married couple were on the faculty of the same institution, the woman couldn't rise above the rank of instructor, even if she was better qualified.

At Ohio University, working with a collaborative circle of innovators, I led the effort to open the doors for women. A diverse group of women came together for mutual support as we moved into "nontraditional" jobs that had been beyond our reach.

I cannot overstate how unprepared I was for that leadership role. I got the job because—as a journalism grad and OU's first female MBA student—I completed a special assignment from the president to write the massive *Report on the Status of Women at Ohio University.*

My report described many problem areas and suggested pressing needs for change, so I had a clear vision of the goals. But I knew *nothing* about university administration, organizational change, or career counseling.

As I moved into this role, I had two go-to approaches. First: call on other women for brainstorming and support. And second: when in doubt, move ahead with sugar grains.

STRUCTURE A FOUR-PART CHANGE PROCESS

During my time in university administration, when I was asked to advise a woman wanting a career shift, my response was often shaped by what I still think of as the "Sugar Grain Process."

Over the decades I've experimented with many variations, but today I still begin a change process with the four basics that worked so well back then. Here is the Sugar Grain way of creating career change:

1. **Develop a vision.** Think freely and optimistically about what you want your life and career to be like—and what you want *yourself* to be like—sometime in the future. If you're considering a big change and your vision is broad,

break it into big goals that provide more definition. For example, if your vision is to work for an international company, your big goals might be to get an MBA, look and feel fit, and become fluent in French.

2. **Identify micro-goals.** A comprehensive vision or a collection of big goals can be so daunting you hesitate to start. Generate momentum by identifying specific small goals that move you in the direction of your big goals. If you have a big fitness goal, your micro-goal might be to walk for twenty minutes, three times a week.

3. **Commit to sugar grains.** Each "sugar grain" is a tiny action that supports a micro-goal. If you plan to start walking, your first grains might be planning your route and buying new shoes. Then each time that you walk even a minute will be another grain.

4. **Record your grains.** This is important: research says you'll make more progress if you not only take the walk but also keep track of it with some kind of log, journal, or app. Noticing a small success leads to more success. And seeing the data that demonstrates your progress can help keep you going.

HOW I TAKE TINY STEPS, AND WHY IT CAN WORK FOR YOU

At any moment, I picture the kind of person I want to be and how I want to live a few years down the road. In my mind's eye I always see a future version of myself. I think of her as "Uber-Bev." She's stronger and more disciplined than I, and she enjoys life.

Once or twice a year I rethink my goals and tweak my Uber-Bev vision. My revised career goals might include something big like a new book proposal or a long-delayed project like improving my accounting system.

Beyond my work, I always have other aspirations, including keeping fit. My approach is to write a brief description of major goals in my journal. Then I push the big picture to the back of my mind and focus on a few specific micro-goals, as well as the little actions—the sugar grains—that will help me reach them.

A three-week micro-goal might be to create the habit of doing yoga for ten minutes a day. For each of twenty-one days I record my sugar grains—the actual minutes of exercise—on a chart in my journal. I've been tracking in different ways since high school, so I have an idea of what works for me. But any recording system can get boring after a while, so I try different methods.

The people most successful at creating change are often the ones who take and keep track of small steps. Here are some reasons why:

1. **Tiny steps are painless.** Beginning something new is often easier if you start small. If a goal feels too difficult, it's tempting to quit, but you can create momentum with little steps. If twenty minutes of walking feels like too much for you, begin with two minutes.

2. **Success fuels success.** Succeeding at something new feels good, even something small like two minutes of walking. You notice progress and your brain rewards you with dopamine. Success motivates you to do it again.

3. **Frequent small steps are habit-forming.** Say you resolve to write a novel and begin by writing for four hours on a Saturday. Chances are you may not be able to carve out another four-hour block for a while, so your resolution could fade away. But if you resolve to write for a manageable fifteen minutes every morning for thirty days, the repetition will help you forge a new habit.

4. **Small steps have no middle.** Starting a new task can be energizing, and finishing a project can feel good. Any activity that goes on for too long, however, becomes boring at the

midpoint. By pursuing steps that are small, you avoid the trap of boredom in the middle.

5. **Tiny steps don't have to be linear.** One reason I often describe little actions as *grains* rather than *steps* is that words like *step* and *path* suggest moving in a straight line. Often your action items can be pretty random. So I might ask a client to do just one daily "thing"—anything at all—to support her job search. That might mean touching base with a former colleague one day, then polishing her LinkedIn profile the next. Keeping up this cadence of unrelated "things" *always* leads to something good.

6. **Little steps shift your identity.** Regularly repeating a small motion can gradually alter how you see yourself. If you start believing in some new aspect of your identity, your behavior will begin to align with your belief. So by the end of a month of working on your novel, you might start thinking of yourself as a writer, which makes you feel more driven to write.

7. **Recording progress feels good.** You're more likely to continue an activity if you feel rewarded. Not only will it feel like a small victory each time you *work* on your novel, but dopamine will help you feel good again when you *record* your minutes of writing.

— KEY TAKEAWAY —

Committing to a course of tiny actions is a smart way to move toward big goals, even when the goals feel so huge they're out of reach. Tracking your grains of action makes the process more powerful.

Chapter 10

Capture the Power of Small Victories

We know structuring a project into a series of small pieces makes it easier to perceive your progress. Because humans often overreact to bad news, it's all too easy to be discouraged by the normal setbacks in a complex assignment. You're more likely to remain enthusiastic if you're able to enjoy little wins along the way.

In this chapter I discuss how little successes impact your happiness in just about any work situation. Teresa Amabile and Steven Kramer have written extensively about how people who experience small but frequent successes are more likely to feel positive and be productive. In a *Harvard Business Review* article, "Small Wins and Feeling Good," they describe how research led them to what they call the "the Progress Principle."

That theory says, "Of all the things that can boost emotions, motivation, and perceptions during a workday, the single most important is making progress on meaningful work."

That doesn't mean you need major victories or breakthroughs. According to Amabile and Kramer, "The good news is that even small wins can boost inner work life tremendously. . . . Even ordinary, incremental progress can increase people's engagement in the work and their happiness during the workday."

This article, aimed at employers, describes to how make work feel meaningful to keep employees motivated, committed, and happy. Its suggestions to managers include setting clear goals, allowing autonomy, providing sufficient resources, and helping with the work.

I like this advice to managers, but this article doesn't offer tips for building the Progress Principle into *your* own job.

A key is that small successes are more likely to boost your mood *if the work itself matters to you.* In other words, the importance you place on the work makes success feel so good. And that raises the question of whether celebrating minor achievements has value if you regard your job as nothing more than a way to pay the rent?

The answer is that you can choose *to infuse meaning into your job—any job—and as you become more fully engaged, your accomplishments will bring you deeper satisfaction.*

That's the view of psychologist Angela Duckworth, who won a MacArthur Fellowship (unofficially known as a "Genius Grant") for her work on how self-control impacts level of achievement.

In her insightful book, *Grit,* Duckworth suggests that no matter where you are, the way you *see* your job is more important than the nature of your occupation. She says *any* job can feel like a calling if you exert effort, play an active role in making your tasks interesting, and cultivate a sense of purpose. By purpose, she means "the intention to contribute to the well-being of others."

Duckworth also suggests that, wherever you are, you can *create more meaning and satisfaction in your work. And that will enhance the impact of your small wins.*

— KEY TAKEAWAY —

A powerful way to cultivate happiness is to structure your work so you can enjoy small but frequent wins. Each little win will matter more if the work itself matters to you.

Chapter 11

Mindfulness Can Help You Feel Calm and Clearheaded

Mindfulness has the potential to impact every major aspect of your work life and enhance every realm of your well-being.

For more than four decades, psychologist Ellen Langer and her Harvard colleagues have been studying the differences between "mindful" and "mindless" activity. They've helped Americans understand how those differences impact the way we live and work.

Since the 1989 publication of Langer's transformative book *Mindfulness*, a vast body of psychological research has filled libraries, captured imaginations, and changed how enlightened managers encourage productivity.

The word *mindfulness* has different meanings, depending on the context. A basic description of being mindful is that you're consciously paying attention, you're in the present moment, and you're not making judgments.

Jon Kabat-Zinn, a renowned author who pioneered mindfulness-based stress reduction, defines it as: "The awareness that arises from paying attention, on purpose, in the present moment and non-judgmentally."

Mindfulness involves being fully present, engaged in what's going on, but not overly reactive. You're calmly aware of what you're doing, but also of your own body, thoughts, and feelings.

I first "got" mindfulness when I read Langer's description of the opposite state: *mindlessness*.

We all engage in mindless activity. Think about a time when you were driving and suddenly realized you had no recollection of the last five miles. Or maybe you lost your glasses, searched frantically, then discovered them resting above your forehead?

Sometimes mindlessness takes the form of automatic behavior, like when you say "excuse me" to a store mannequin, or you type notes at a meeting without really processing what you're hearing. You may notice when other people are mindless, like the waiter who repeats the specials by rote but doesn't seem to hear your questions.

According to Langer, mindlessness is widespread in the workplace and can have devastating consequences. When we're mindless on the job:

1. **We don't spot developments that should trigger action.** Our understanding of the environment is frozen, and we're oblivious to little changes that should alert us that it's time to pursue an opportunity or take corrective steps to avoid a disaster.

2. **Our judgment and performance are compromised.** Our lack of awareness can show up as prejudice, rigidity, or an unwillingness to consider new ideas or recognize the strengths of other people. And it makes us more likely to drift into fatigue, conflict, or burnout.

3. **We can't solve problems.** Our disengagement dulls our ability to find solutions, and so we might underachieve or start feeling unnecessarily helpless.

4. **We make a poor impression.** Research says when our mind is wandering, we come across to other people as unintelligent and even unattractive.

On the other hand, Langer says that being *mindful* on the job "may increase flexibility, productivity, innovation, leadership ability, and satisfaction."

When we're mindful, we engage in whatever is going on in front of us and focus on the tasks at hand. This is essential because unexpected developments arise in any workplace. A mindful worker can manage problems as they come up, calmly handling them as part of the ongoing process.

When we're mindful on the job:

1. **We notice.** We remain sensitive to small ways in which our situation is changing, and we act accordingly.

2. **We're centered.** We feel balanced and fully aware, rather than depressed, bored, or disconnected. We often feel pretty good because mindfulness isn't stressful and it allows us to be happily engaged in what we're doing.

3. **We're not judgmental.** We recognize that no single perspective explains a situation, and we remain open and curious.

4. **We appear attractive and authentic.** Other people—and even animals—sense that we are present and trustworthy, and our colleagues are likely to see us as genuine and charismatic.

5. **We're better leaders.** We fully engage in conversations, we recognize others' strengths, and we provide effective positive reinforcement.

— KEY TAKEAWAY —

When you're mindful, you are both calm and alert, living in the moment, enjoying a state of focused relaxation. Becoming more mindful can transform your work life and enhance your whole life.

Chapter 12

Neuroscience Has Made Mindfulness a Hot Topic

In the years since Dr. Langer's first book, neuroscience has changed our understanding of the brain and shed light on the tight connection between our body and mind. *A critical finding is that anything you do or don't do in the normal course of your life can alter your brain for better or worse.*

Scientists have found that because of its "neuroplasticity," your brain, like your body, changes itself in response to its experience. Depending on what's going on with you, your brain can modify its structure, increase or reduce its size, or shift its biochemistry.

According to *Altered Traits* co-author Daniel Goleman, by undertaking mindfulness exercises, you can improve your brain's fitness level, much like doing reps with weights develops your biceps. The benefits of a serious mindfulness exercise program include reduced stress, stronger social relationships, better control over your emotions, lower blood pressure, and enhanced attention and decision-making capacity.

The most prominent tool for developing mindfulness is meditation, an ancient practice now recognized for supporting mindfulness long after you've completed your meditative exercise.

The benefits of meditation and other mindfulness activities have caught the attention of businesses, schools, and other organizations that recognize the impact of well-being. Some now provide quiet rooms or offer in-house mindfulness classes. Their goals include supporting mental health, promoting a positive culture, and enhancing productivity.

By adopting a mindfulness practice, you can enhance your ability to manage your own thought processes. For example, you can develop the skill, known as "diffusion," of putting yourself at a distance from your thoughts as they come and go. You're practicing that technique when a worry or disturbing memory floats into your mind while you're meditating, and you gently tell it to move along, instead of being overcome by a need to act.

Another skill is "expansion," which allows your emotions to bubble up without grabbing away your control. The idea is that you don't try to suppress your feelings. Instead, you notice and accept them, allowing them to come and go without a struggle. The concept of "expanding" suggests you make room for your emotions, releasing tension and simply observing them.

THERE ARE MANY WAYS TO START A MINDFULNESS PRACTICE

Goleman says that just like when you take up a sport, finding a meditative practice and sticking with it has the greatest benefits. The more you practice, the more you benefit. His advice is to identify a meditative approach worth trying, then decide how long "you can realistically practice daily—even as short as a few minutes—(and) try it for a month and see how you feel after those thirty days."

Over the last twenty years I've been to various classes on meditation, read about it, and practiced a number of contemplative techniques. I must confess that, despite sporadic efforts, I've never been able to commit to a dedicated ritual, like meditating for fifteen minutes at the same time and place each morning.

Somehow, despite my failure to create a consistent daily meditation practice, I've built a variety of mindfulness activities into my life. I frequently repeat a traditional mantra in my mind, and now it tends to pop into my head at the first sign of trouble or worry. I do some yoga. I often pause for a few deep breaths. Almost every day I walk outside, without earbuds, noticing what's going on with nature.

I'm not sure how it has come together, but my patchwork of mini-exercises has made a difference in my life. I'm calmer, happier, and healthier than I used to be, and I don't get bored.

At the same time, I see how mindfulness routines make a difference for some of my clients. Clearing their mental clutter and enhancing their focus help them be more relaxed yet still engaged at work. When a client is in the midst of crisis, I find it can be helpful to start our session with a brief breathing exercise, so we can let go of stress and bring our best selves into the conversation.

There are abundant forms of meditation, and I can't guess which ones might work for you. But I urge you to explore approaches that seem appealing. It's easy to search online, select books, locate classes, or download apps.

EXERCISE:

To practice mindfulness right now, try one of these techniques:

1. **Breathe.** Pause and sit tall but comfortably in your chair. Close your eyes. Notice where in your body you feel tension, like your neck, jaw, or shoulders. Roll your shoulders or wiggle your jaw to release that tension. Now take at least five slow, deep breaths, expanding your belly as you draw in the air. Notice how your breath feels as you inhale through your nose and exhale through your mouth. If thoughts come to mind, just let them go and refocus on your breath. Open your eyes slowly.

2. **Go for a mindful walk.** Go for a slow stroll, noticing the details of the world around you as you move along. If possible, go outside and— even if you're in a city—watch for signs of nature. Look carefully at a tree, bird, or cloud, and take note of shapes and colors.

3. **Take a lunch or coffee break.** Leave the spot where you work, find a comfortable place to sit, and take a few minutes to eat or drink something. Instead of looking at your phone, observe the color and texture of your foods. Savor tastes and chew carefully. Notice what your beverage feels like as it flows down your throat.

4. **Find a guide.** Go to YouTube, Spotify, or other apps and search for "guided meditations." Listen to the voice and follow the speaker's instructions about relaxing your body and letting go of distractions. If unrelated thoughts float into your mind, let them go and refocus on the voice.

Chapter 13

Learn from Ben Franklin, America's First Self-Help Guru

The person who may deserve the most credit for building a passion for self-improvement into the national culture is US "founding father" Ben Franklin.

In his splendid biography *Benjamin Franklin,* Walter Isaacson writes that Franklin was "America's best scientist, inventor, diplomat, writer and business strategist," as well as a practical political thinker.

Beyond Franklin's popular inventions, like the lightning rod and bifocals, Isaacson says, "the most interesting thing that Franklin invented, and continually reinvented, was himself. America's first great publicist, he was, in his life and in his writings, consciously trying to create a new American archetype . . . Partly, it was a matter of image . . . But the image he created was rooted in reality."

The nation's first wildly popular self-help book was the *Autobiography of Benjamin Franklin,* a posthumously published collection of Franklin's papers. Franklin described the work as his "memoirs," but at least one of his goals was instructing his fellow citizens about how to achieve their full potential.

The book describes how Franklin, with less than three years of formal schooling, as a teenager taught himself to write and speak well. He read essays in leading English journals, took brief notes, and then later recreated the essays in his own words.

Franklin also describes how, in 1732, he first published *Poor Richard's Almanack*, which is best remembered for the maxims scattered throughout each annual issue. During the twenty-five years of *Almanacks*, Franklin borrowed wisdom from the classics and restated it in pithy, succinct prose. He shared his philosophy of self-management with gems like these:

- "Eat to live, and not live to eat."
- "Haste makes waste."
- "Diligence is the mother of good luck."

When I first read his book as a teenager, I was struck by how, in 1729, twenty-year-old Franklin attempted to systemically shape certain of his standards of behavior. He undertook a "bold and arduous Project of arriving at moral Perfection."

To structure this self-help project, and as part of his "plan for self-examination," Franklin created a book for keeping track of his efforts to develop thirteen "virtues," including

- **Order:** "Let all your things have their places; let each part of your business have its time."
- **Frugality:** "Make no expense but to do good to others or yourself; i.e., waste nothing."
- **Industry:** "Lose no time; be always employed in something useful; cut off all unnecessary actions."
- **Sincerity:** "Use no hurtful deceit; think innocently and justly, and, if you speak, speak accordingly."

What most intrigued me then were the charts that served as Franklin's report card. To start, he used red ink to draw vertical lines that created seven columns on each page, one for each day of the week. Across the columns he drew thirteen lines, one for each virtue. In each day's column he made black marks to note "every fault I found upon examination to have been committed respecting that virtue upon that day." His virtuous weeks were recorded as a "clean book."

Franklin continued his recordkeeping, with some gaps, for a year and then gradually stopped. Speaking of these early efforts, he said he eventually realized perfection cannot be attained. Nevertheless, he felt better and happier for trying.

The year after his self-examination exercise, Franklin created a model of how self-improvement can be more successful if you have a diverse support group. He formed a "club of mutual improvement," known as the "JUNTO," that met every Friday night for many years. Members discussed moral and political issues and undertook civic projects, like creation of the city's first subscription library. They also helped each other's businesses.

Part of what makes the *Autobiography* so intriguing is that Franklin comes across as a flawed person. He struggled with many "virtues," like temperance and chastity. But he faced up to some of his flaws and persevered in his efforts to get better. Franklin kept learning and reaffirming what Isaacson describes as his "sincere belief in leading a virtuous life."

— KEY TAKEAWAY —

Franklin teaches us that self-improvement—which means moving closer to the life you want to live and the person you choose to be—requires effort, persistence, and the ability to learn from mistakes. But you can do it. We all can choose to live a life closer to our ideal.

The search for self-improvement is nothing new, but we now have a wealth of new information about the workings of our minds and our bodies. The scientific knowledge developed in just the last few years would blow Ben Franklin's mind.

Chapter 14

Change Things Up by Managing Your Habits

A theme throughout this book is making your work life more satisfying by acting mindfully, focusing attention on the important things, and making conscious choices.

Let's face it, though: *making decisions can wear you out.* Your brain has only so much stamina for deciding things. When your energy has been drained after hours of problem solving, it's no wonder you can't make the little choices that pop up at the end of your day.

Our lives are so complicated that it's amazing we get along as well as we do. If you don't work from home, simply getting up, preparing to leave, and commuting to work can bring plenty of decision points.

The reason we aren't exhausted by routine choices, like turning left or right on a familiar drive, is that we glide through much of life on automatic pilot. *Our conscious minds don't have to actually evaluate options like the best routes to work because our habits take over.*

Habits are learned routines we follow automatically, without having to think about them. Our minds naturally create habits that allow our nonconscious selves to take charge, giving our conscious selves a rest.

Our good habits help us effortlessly make positive choices. Often they guide us as we select food, prepare for tasks, and complete routine projects. But sometimes our habits are not so good, and they put us in the wrong groove.

My client Julie, a thirty-something single lawyer, wanted more control over her life. She said too much of her time revolved around the needs of other people, particularly her boss and the clients of the nonprofit where she worked. She was struggling to catch up on paperwork. In her personal life she felt out of shape, disorganized, often lonely, and frequently exhausted. She couldn't seem to get it together to make a change.

When we first spoke, Julie blamed others for the chaos in her life. However, as she described her daily routines, she noticed that her own habits were part of the problem. For example, after a long and stressful day at work, she typically grabbed junk food and collapsed in front of the TV. In the morning, after staying up watching talk shows, she'd arrive at her desk feeling tired and less organized than ever.

To develop a more detailed picture of her patterns, Julie decided to keep a meticulous time log. For several weeks she recorded her activities, making notes about how she used every waking hour. The results helped her create a slate of goals intended to support a happier, more productive life.

One goal was to develop more energy by adopting a better sleep schedule. That meant challenging her habit of mindlessly watching late night shows. Julie didn't want to give up her TV programs cold turkey, so we talked about creating new habits gradually, one "sugar grain at a time."

To start, she elected to set an alarm to chime at midnight. Her plan was to immediately click off her program, then note her actual TV shutoff time on a spreadsheet. Julie stuck with her plan during the first week. Then each week for several months she set the alarm for a slightly earlier time and faithfully tracked her media click-off time. Eventually, on most weeknights, Julie was turning off her screens at 11:00.

As Julie started sleeping better, she began building or altering other habits, from her food choices to the way she tidied her desk and managed her calendar. At the end of the nine-month coaching program, Julie hadn't reached all her goals, but she felt good and was upbeat about the future. She had learned *how* to better manage the habits that shape her daily life.

Most exciting, Julie noticed that when she created new habits in one part of her life, she was more energetic and creative in other areas. This fueled her desire to continue the change process. Two years later she wrote me to describe how she'd kept up her efforts and eventually won a big promotion, lost ten pounds, and expanded her social circle.

IMPROVE YOUR DAYS BY ADJUSTING YOUR HABITS

Even without trying, you've already instinctively shaped your lifestyle by forming habits. You're so used to them that you don't give them a thought. Many have value and save you from dithering over minor choices, like when to brush your teeth or where to put your groceries.

If you step back and watch yourself for a day, you'll notice a number of habits that shape much of your time. You might observe that you always prepare your morning coffee in the same way. You go through the same routine when you start your work. Or after dinner you automatically walk your dog around the same blocks.

While many habits are useful, chances are some of your work habits waste your time or drain your energy. For example, many people start the day reading low-priority emails for an hour or more, no matter how many high-priority projects await their attention.

You can identify habits that don't serve you well, and also spot ways to improve your normal routines, by recording your activities for a week or so, like Julie did. One option is to create a spreadsheet with a column for each day and a row for each hour. Then jot down all that you do in each hourly block. If you're like my clients, you'll be surprised by which activities are using up much of your time.

Another method for getting a new perspective is to make notes in your journal as you go through the day. However you record your observations, the goal is to step back and develop a fresh, accurate view of your customary behavior. The next step is to make better use of your time by shifting unproductive habits.

A good way to exercise more control over your habits is to experiment with creating new ones. As with many changes, starting with something small can help.

As you consider a possible new habit, visualize it as a three-step loop:

1. **A habit starts with a cue,** which acts as the trigger stimulating the behavior you want to establish. A cue might be a certain time of day, your running shoes placed at the door, or anything else that reminds you of the activity you intend to establish as an automatic routine. Julie's trigger was the alarm that reminded her to turn off her TV.

2. **The routine** is the activity that you want to do automatically. In Julie's case that was clicking off the screen.

3. **The reward** is something that helps you feel good about the routine. The instant Julie wrote her switch-off time on her spreadsheet, she felt a sense of accomplishment that served as her immediate reward. The next morning she tried to pause and notice how it felt to wake up from a good night's sleep.

EXERCISE:

Experiment with creating a small new habit. Think about your life over the last few days and consider how it might have been a little better. Notice some element that you would like to improve, and think of a specific habit that could lead to improvement.

To illustrate, say that you want to feel more upbeat at the end of your workdays. So you choose to create the habit of ending each day by writing a quick list of three things that went well.

This could be your habit loop:

1. **Your cue** might be completing an end-of-work task or shutting down your laptop.

2. **The routine** could be picking up your journal and writing your three-item success list.

3. **The reward** includes feeling better about the day and experiencing satisfaction at the sight of your journal entry.

Over time, your habit loop will come more naturally. Your brain will reinforce your reward by generating tiny shots of feel-good chemicals, like dopamine, when you complete the routine. As your habit becomes engrained, dopamine will flow not only when you *enjoy* the reward but also when you *anticipate* it. You'll look forward to writing your list.

Chapter 15

Create Better Habits

Dysfunctional habits can hold you back. Maybe it's time to make your job more satisfying by examining your current routines, creating new habits, and reshaping old ones.

It's not hard to create the cue-routine-reward loop for establishing a stand-alone habit like hanging your keys on a hook by the door. Your cue could be a sticky note near your entrance, the routine is putting your key ring on the hook, and the reward is feeling organized when you arrive and leave home.

In real life habits get complicated. New routines compete with old ones, like putting your keys in your pocket. And immediate satisfaction often outweighs the promise of long-term benefits, like when your desire to lose weight by ordering salads isn't powerful enough to overcome your craving for pizza.

Reminding yourself of the person you want to become can reinforce your commitment to new habits. For example, if you want to be respected as a conscientious, well-organized professional, you might decide to build habits that help you be more punctual. As you work on a specific routine, like leaving your desk on time, your sense of achievement can be enhanced by noticing that you're behaving like the organized person you want to become.

Transforming the habits that shape your life takes effort, but you can do it bit by bit. Your determination to create the life you want will help you keep getting up again each time you stumble. If you're ready to create new habits, these strategies will help:

1. **Break challenges into *little* habits.** To create a major shift, break your goals into manageable pieces. If your objective is to get more exercise, you might start with the habit of doing ten minutes of stretching each morning. Identify "sugar grains" and pinch them off, little by little.

2. **Be specific.** In *Atomic Habits,* author James Clear emphasizes the importance of creating a detailed vision of the habit you intend to create. He says, "People who make a specific plan for when and where they will perform a new habit are more likely to follow through . . . Many people think they lack motivation when what they really lack is clarity."

3. **Repeat, repeat, repeat.** You get the full value from a habit that's so programmed you do it without thinking, like shutting the door when you leave home. Predicting how many repetitions it will take to create a pattern that's so engrained is difficult because it depends on many factors, like what you're tackling, how much you want it, and what barriers you face. But the more reps you do, the more instinctive your habit will become.

4. **Try physical cues.** Cues you see and touch are powerful reminders that it's time to do your thing. I often place objects in strategic places to help me stay on track. One challenge of traveling is having work tools where I need them. I still use some paper notes and hardbound books and journals, so I've created habits to assure I always have the ones I want. Before a trip, as I finish working with items, I gradually store them in a tote. The night before I head out, I put the tote by the door, so I can't leave without tripping over it.

5. **Keep track.** *My clients who are most successful at habit building are the ones who track their progress.* Whether

you use an app, a chart, or your journal, it's important to precisely state your objective and record your steps in that direction. If you miss a day, make a notation explaining why. Your recording system will keep you focused and provide feedback about what is or isn't working.

6. **Think about it.** You can reinforce a new pattern not only by performing the behavior but also by just *thinking* about doing it. As often as possible, remind yourself of your intention to keep up your new habit. Imagine what it will be like when you next perform the routine.

7. **Anticipate obstacles.** While you're creating a habit, you may be tempted to skip some reps. A voice in your head may say things like, "I don't have time," or, "Missing one day won't hurt." Prepare for these challenges by thinking about ways your habit building has been successful in the past. Then create backup plans for times when life interferes with your routine. For example, your plan for particularly frantic mornings could be to schedule a brief yoga break later in the day.

8. **Find support.** You will be more likely to maintain your positive habits if you spend time with people who have the same value system and can support your goals. According to Clear, your culture sets your expectation for what is normal. He says, "Surround yourself with people who have the habits you want to have yourself." Keeping up your fitness habits is easier if you have friends who regularly go to the gym. Buddy systems contribute to the success of people struggling with serious addictions, including through programs like Alcoholics Anonymous.

9. **Stack new habits on old ones.** An easy way to create a habit is to attach it to one you already have. This worked for Anika, a harried IT service manager who craved more

control over her time. All day people sought her help, and often she'd drop everything to respond and then lose track of her priorities. I suggested she start work a little earlier to plan her schedule and assure time for important projects. At first Anika was reluctant to give up the thirty minutes she spent enjoying her breakfast latte at a favorite coffee shop. Then she realized she could make her latte habit the basis of a new routine. Now each day at the coffee shop she reviews her calendar and "to-do" list and decides how to organize a successful day.

TACKLE A BAD HABIT BY REPLACING IT WITH A BETTER ONE

Breaking a long-held habit is not easy. Often, instead of trying to quit a destructive habit, a better approach is to replace it with a new, more positive routine. *New York Times* reporter Charles Duhigg wrote *The Power of Habit*, my favorite book about habit building. He says, "Change might not be fast and it isn't always easy. But with time and effort, almost any habit can be reshaped."

To illustrate his four-part framework for changing habits, Duhigg describes how he shook his unhealthy, fattening routine of buying a chocolate chip cookie every afternoon in the office cafeteria:

- **Step one: Identify the negative routine.** Duhigg wanted to quit his habit of getting up from his desk, walking to the cafeteria, buying the cookie, and eating it while chatting with friends.
- **Step two: Experiment with rewards.** Rewards satisfy the cravings that trigger the bad routine, but sometimes the true reward might not be obvious. After some trial and error, Duhigg realized that what he craved more than food was an opportunity to hang with friends.

- **Step three: Isolate the cue.** Duhigg realized his trigger was the time of day. Every afternoon at 3:30 he felt an urge to go to the cafeteria for his cookie.
- **Step four: Plan a replacement routine.** Once he identified his cue (the time) and his reward (the chatting), Duhigg looked around for an alternative to his old routine. Recognizing he wanted company more than cookies, he made this plan: "At 3:30 every day, I will walk to a friend's desk and talk for 10 minutes." Initially he set an alarm for 3:30 to remind himself to take a walk. But he said by the time he was writing his book, "at about 3:30 every day, I absent-mindedly stand up, look around the newsroom for someone to talk to, spend ten minutes gossiping about the news, and then go back to my desk. It occurs almost without me thinking about it. It has become a habit."

— KEY TAKEAWAY —

Examining and reshaping some of the habits that frame your daily life can be an effective and interesting way to create positive change gradually, over time.

The more you get your head in the game, the more successful you will be at managing your habits. Your tracking logs and journals are tools that will help. As with any change process, writing about your goals, gathering data, examining the challenges and pitfalls, and envisioning the benefits of success will help keep you on track.

Chapter 16

Improve Each Day by Cultivating Gratitude

Are you ready to practice building a positive new habit? Consider the powerful habit of ending each day by writing about three things that went well.

Sometimes my clients are skeptical about gratitude exercises. I understand that. Suggesting that you'll feel better if you pay more attention to the good things in your life might seem too glib, too cute, too simplistic.

People resist advice about the value of feeling grateful for other reasons also. Maybe a parent tried to make them feel guilty for not being thankful. Or perhaps it strikes them as tempting fate.

In the past I hesitated to focus too much on the good things in my life. It felt unwise to remind the Universe that I had more than my share of abundance. That changed almost twenty years ago when my husband bounced back from cancer. Suddenly, the floodgates flew open and my gratitude flowed without restraint. I woke up feeling grateful, and the feeling translated into a sensation of well-being throughout the day.

Since then, I've enjoyed practicing gratitude and am intrigued by the power of this quiet emotion to help keep life on an even keel. Increasingly, I've used it as a coaching tool. Research shows that generating heartfelt gratitude is a quick way to spark a more positive attitude and boost your physical and mental health.

Gratitude is the positive emotion you feel when you contemplate gifts or benefits you've received, or you think about people and things you appreciate. It's tied to noticing the goodness in your life while also recognizing that a source of that goodness is something beyond yourself.

Psychologist Robert Emmons, an expert on gratitude, says that feeling grateful is healthy not only for your mind and body but also for your relationships. In a series of studies, Emmons and his colleagues asked subjects to keep gratitude journals for just three weeks. He says the results were "overwhelming." Among other benefits, people who kept the journals experienced

- Stronger immune systems
- Lower blood pressure
- Fewer aches and pains
- Better sleep
- A sense of being alert and alive
- More joy and optimism
- Feelings of compassion and forgiveness

Other studies suggest gratitude actually causes your brain to change. When you're actively engaged in appreciation, certain threatening messages and anxious instincts are cut off from your brain's neocortex. For this reason, it's impossible for your brain to register fear at the same time it's experiencing appreciation.

By focusing on things you appreciate and cultivating gratitude, you can quiet your anxiety and at the same time stimulate confidence, patience, and positive energy. Gratitude can simultaneously calm you and strengthen your sense of self-worth. It helps you heal from trauma and build resistance.

One function of gratitude seems to be helping humans form bonds with other humans. When we appreciate a person's thoughtful gesture, we are more likely to reach out to them. Feeling grateful also causes us to be more honest, generous, and self-controlled when we interact with others.

EXPLORE THE POWER OF GRATITUDE WITH THESE TECHNIQUES

Sometimes finding a sense of thankfulness is not easy. Experiencing gratitude seems to run counter to several human tendencies, like the way we overrespond to negative cues, and our desire to feel responsible for our own destiny.

Although you may have to regularly nudge yourself toward gratitude, it's worth the effort. The more you practice, the easier it gets.

Here are just a few ways to trigger your sense of feeling grateful:

1. **Make choices.** A feeling of gratitude can start with your *intention* to adjust your attitude and reframe how you look at life's developments. You can *choose* gratitude by refocusing your attention on the best parts of any situation, even when you're in crisis.

2. **Make lists.** You can stimulate feelings of gratitude by recording things you appreciate. In the context of your job, your list might include the tasks you like best and the good things your paycheck allows you to buy for your family. In your journal, list things that make you feel thankful, whether a lovely sunset or a friend's kindness.

3. **Keep rereading.** Look at your gratitude list often. The practice may calm your worries, help break the loop of your repetitive negative thoughts, and lift your spirits.

4. **Change your consciousness.** Meditation techniques incorporating feelings of gratitude can boost your confidence

and help you focus on the positive. One study suggests you can enhance the rhythm and strength of your heartbeat by concentrating on something you deeply appreciate while you also visualize a calming energy flowing directly into your heart.

5. **Offer thanks.** If you thank others for what they do, they'll feel better and so will you. Perfunctory comments don't work nearly as well as expressions of gratitude that you really mean. So when you express your thanks, take a second to actually focus on the benefit you received.

6. **Pray.** For many people prayer is a wonderful way to enter a state of thankfulness. This is true even when people aren't sure they believe in God.

— KEY TAKEAWAY —

Gratitude enhances our well-being, empowers us to connect with other people, and often triggers an upward spiral of positive emotion. In our hectic lives, feelings of gratitude can easily slip away, but there are numerous ways to cultivate thankfulness and its many benefits.

Chapter 17

Enjoying Your Free Time Helps You Thrive at Work

Sometimes the best way to generate new on-the-job energy is to disconnect for a while and have a little fun. Whether you're playing sports or playing music, growing veggies or cooking them, enjoying your favorite leisure activity is an excellent way to recover from career stress and stimulate new creativity.

Eminent psychologist Daniel Goleman describes the restorative power of serious leisure in his book *Focus*. He says our work life in the modern world is exhausting us because information overload complicates the demands of getting something done. Because we're constantly sorting out the important info from the irrelevant, we have to work extra hard. And that's tiring.

Goleman says, "Tightly focused attention gets fatigued—much like an overworked muscle—when we push to the point of cognitive exhaustion." The results include "a drop in effectiveness and a rise in distractedness and irritability."

To remain at your healthy, energetic best, it's wise to psychologically detach from work when you find yourself dragging. Even if you love what you do, both your mind and body need to regularly move away from the challenges of your job. They need time to rest and reboot.

"We do well to unplug regularly," says Goleman. The way we spend our down time matters. The best option is an immersive experience where "positive absorption shuts off the inner voice, that running dialogue with ourselves that goes on even during our quiet moments."

Other researchers agree your work life will be more satisfying if you pursue hobbies in your free time. You're more likely to thrive if you regularly step away from your job and earnestly pursue some fun. But that doesn't mean curling up on the couch. *The benefits of leisure come from throwing yourself into activities that feel like play.*

People who regularly enjoy pastimes tend to be healthier and happier. Becoming absorbed in various hobbies can help you grow in different ways. Workers with creative outlets unrelated to their profession tend to be better at solving problems and breaking new ground once they return to work.

If your favorite pastime is artistic—whether painting a picture or knitting a sweater—you're more likely to innovate on the job. If your leisure activity is challenging—whether you ride your bike for a hundred miles or invent an app—your struggle helps you become resilient and confident.

As long as it is not passive, like watching videos, any hobby can be energizing. One reason it is so stimulating is that *you are the one who chose it*. You don't take it up because someone says so, or you think it's good for your image. You do this because it's fun and you get totally into it, forgetting about your worries.

THIS BUSY CAREER EXPERT GETS ENERGY FROM HER FREE TIME

One friend whose thriving career is supported by her hobby is work and finance expert Kerry Hannon*. She is a prolific author of books like *Great Pajama Jobs*, a keynote speaker, and a columnist for media organizations like the *New York Times* and the *Wall Street Journal*.

Kerry seems to be constantly in the news, speaking at conferences, testifying before Congress, and turning out a steady flow of influential articles. It's hard to imagine how she does it all.

When she was the first guest on my *Jazzed About Work* podcast, Kerry explained how her favorite free time activity helps her remain grounded, energetic, and upbeat. Riding horses is Kerry's passion, and she has been doing it since she was six years old.

Kerry doesn't just hack around. She regularly competes and wins blue ribbons in challenging AA-rated hunter and jumper shows. In these events, the horse jumps over a series of fences while maintaining a smooth stride and excellent form. It's like horse and rider are joined in a choreographed, flowing dance.

Here are four ways Kerry's passion for horses supports her busy work life:

1. **It keeps her centered.** Kerry loves being outdoors, looking at the countryside, particularly when she's with horses and dogs. Research says people are hardwired to release anxiety when they spend time with animals and in nature. More than that, Kerry finds something almost mystical about working closely with a horse. She says, "Horsemanship is about caring for another living being and accepting accountability and responsibility for another life. And that is magic."

2. **It reduces stress.** Kerry says that being with horses is *her* time. It's "incredibly freeing" and "the ultimate de-stressor." She says, "Earth people don't know what it's like. . . . You can't think about anything but what you're doing when you're on a thousand-pound animal. . . . Riding requires, and, in fact, demands total focus."

3. **It makes her a tougher competitor.** Kerry is more entrepreneurial because of her experience in the horse world. She once told me, "In many ways, setting goals and developing the inner tools to grind it out during rough patches

to achieve at this level are transferable to other parts of my work and personal life." She says that to succeed at shows you must be positive, have a plan, and be prepared for the unexpected.

4. **It spurs hard work.** In the podcast, Kerry explained that horses are expensive, so they provide a financial motivation to work harder. She puts aside some of her earnings "to spend on rich experiences. . . . For me that's about being around a horse. . . . So I'll equate a new assignment I get with Brinkley's board bill. It becomes a barter system in my brain—if I do this extra assignment, my hobby is paid for."

Kerry's riding is an example of the immersive experience that Goleman describes, where you're totally absorbed and nothing else is on your mind. Not many of us have interests that we love with the intensity that Kerry adores riding. Yet we each have the potential to find entertaining pastimes that lift our moods, allow us to grow, and help us recover from the demands and challenges at work.

— KEY TAKEAWAY —

You can recover from stress and find fresh energy by regularly stepping away from your job and devoting time to activities you enjoy. Don't think that grinding away endlessly at your work assignments is a smart career move. You will perform better if you build rest and variety into your life.

Chapter 18

Feel Better by Spending
Time in Nature

I've loved Washington since my days as a law student. Part of
what makes this city so special is the array of options for getting
outdoors and connecting with nature. The city has tree-lined
streets and wonderful paths for strolling, from the majestic National Mall to the wooded trails of Rock Creek Park and the
dozens of public gardens.

Much as I enjoy the natural beauty spread across this city,
my long-term goal always was to have a home in the country.
During the toughest days of my career, I distracted myself with
garden books and fantasized about whole days spent walking
dogs off leash and digging in the dirt.

I pushed hard, my husband was agreeable, and in the '90s we
bought a fixer-upper farmhouse about eighty miles from DC, in
rural Rappahannock County, Virginia.

Now it's our primary home, but for years Andy and I shifted
between hectic, job-focused weekdays in DC and more relaxed
weekends working around the country property and spending
long hours outdoors.

Like other weekenders, we soon noticed how we all—including our frequent city-dweller houseguests—are so much *nicer*
once we're in the country. Arriving guests might bustle in with
briefcases bulging with office work, saying how they expected
to work all weekend. But once they took a walk or settled onto

a porch, their perspectives shifted and they seemed to become more relaxed, patient versions of themselves.

I know the personality change comes partly because the pressures of daily life are eighty miles away. But there's more to it. You can see people's personalities soften a bit after a few hours outdoors.

In recent decades scientists have documented that even a little time in nature does, in fact, go a long way toward making people feel happier and healthier. When you take walks in a natural environment, you let go of stress and your negative thoughts may fade away.

It's important to realize you don't have to head to a rural area to enjoy the benefits of nature. In one UK study, researchers found that people who spent *just two hours* a week in parks or other local green spaces are much more likely to report good health and well-being than those who don't.

Also, there's evidence that being outdoors can make you a kinder, more generous person. Studies suggest being in nature helps you feel more trusting, helpful, and caring toward other people. Other research finds that when children feel connected to a natural space they also feel more altruistic and protective of the environment.

One theory about the power of being outdoors is that humans are born with a "unity consciousness." In other words, we have an inborn sense of being connected with nature and the Earth, and getting in touch with that connection can soothe much of what ails us.

While there are different theories about why contact with the natural world is so powerful, there's no doubt it can be good for us. As long as we feel safe, time in nature can reduce our anxiety, lower our blood pressure, enhance our resilience and self-esteem, and promote a more positive mood.

CONNECTING WITH NATURE
CAN HELP YOU FLOURISH AT WORK

Spending time in a natural environment can promote your well-being and help you manage on-the-job pressures. Even a brief walk across a park might boost your workday. Here are some options:

1. **Care for a garden.** You may get healthier by raising your own organic vegetables. And proponents of "horticulture therapy" say gardening supports wellness regardless of where or what you grow. They suggest it can promote healing and lead to more positive social interaction for people with physical or mental illness. Some workplace studies suggest simply bringing green plants into an office environment can increase productivity and facilitate positive relations among workers.

2. **Get a pet.** There's evidence that engaging with animals—even by simply filling bird feeders—can lower our blood pressure and our cholesterol. Most pet owners understand the healing power of time spent with a beloved dog or cat, and trained companion animals are helping people to recover from medical challenges.

3. **Drive calmly.** Highway researchers have found that drivers' blood pressure, heart rate, and other stress indicators are reduced when they pass through green areas. Viewing nature from the driver's seat seems to decrease anger and anxiety, enhance attention and interest, and increase feelings of pleasure.

4. **Consider biophilic building design.** *Biophilia* is a term for humans' inherent love for nature. Architects interested in sustainable design argue it should influence how buildings are designed. For example, allowing better access to sunlight can improve workers' mood and productivity. When

hospital patients have window views of grass and trees, they heal more quickly.

5. **Take a walk.** Being outside is great, but walking outside is even better. When you move your body, the repetitive nature of taking steps can be calming. In *The Joy of Movement*, psychologist Kelly McGonigal says that within a few minutes of outdoor activity people report major mood shifts. She says, "They don't just feel better—they feel different, somehow both distanced from the problems of everyday life and more connected to life itself." A walk with friends or colleagues may offer additional benefits because people who exercise together outdoors seem to bond in a special way.

6. **Spark creativity.** Through the ages, people have seen walking as a way to stimulate fresh ideas. My youngest sister, Libby Vick, says, "As a longtime community college professor I've adapted my course materials and activities many times as I adjusted to changing student demographics and revised curriculum. Every single idea I've developed from scratch has occurred while taking a long walk alone with my dog. Sometimes I'll work through a complex idea over several days of walking. Sitting in front of a computer is never the same because the creative process is interrupted by too many other thoughts. When I'm outside, those other thoughts gradually disappear and my mind is free to create."

— KEY TAKEAWAY —

Spending even a little time in nature can make you feel happier and more relaxed and give you fresh energy for work. Just being outside for a while can do you good, and regularly walking outside can boost your health.

Chapter 19

Managing Your Attention Is a Basic Skill

In the early 1970s, California tennis teacher Timothy Gallwey noticed that his students improved more quickly when he stopped telling them what to do. Instead, he helped them relax and found they were better at hitting the ball.

If you search online for "The Reasoner Report, Inner Game of Tennis," you'll find a fuzzy video of Gallwey teaching tennis to a random group of beginners. Filmed as a TV news segment, this classic video clip seems like it started as an expose of ridiculous teaching claims. But it ended up as evidence of Gallwey's successful "inner tennis" technique of assisting students to acquire tennis skills once their minds relax into a state of "nonjudgmental awareness."

Gallwey described his learning process as a matter of "trial and self-correction." The idea is to let your body do what it can do naturally, but you "have to put your mind somewhere where it can remain calm" because it wants to interfere.

ABC News host Harry Reasoner described one volunteer student, Molly, as "a somewhat sedentary middle-aged lady." She wore a long, loose dress rather than sports gear, and said she "hadn't done anything athletic in, like, twenty years."

Gallwey first asked Molly to stand on his side of the court and watch the trajectory of the ball his assistant was sending gently over the net for him to return. He asked her to say "bounce" each time the ball hit the court and "hit" the instant it touched his racket. Gallwey was modeling tennis movements and encouraging Molly to match his rhythm. Once she was closely watching the ball, her conscious mind was too occupied to allow any nagging inner voice to interrupt her learning.

As soon as Molly had picked up the rhythm of the ball, Gallwey told her to start returning it whenever she felt ready. And she did.

In about ten minutes Molly was smoothly volleying, hitting both forehand and backhand. Shortly after the seventeen-minute mark, she learned to serve.

In a voice heard over the footage of her playing tennis, Molly said returning the ball had felt effortless. She was doing "what came naturally," but every time she did start to think, "things went wrong."

Gallwey explained his approach in *The Inner Game of Tennis.* Then he went on to reach millions of people with a groundbreaking series of *Inner* books and videos, all describing how to overcome barriers by quieting the conscious mind and quietly focusing attention.

I was hugely influenced by *The Inner Game of Work,* published in 1999. That was around the time I first thought of taking up coaching and was puzzling over what makes some people so much more successful than others. Before then, I don't believe I had a sense that *attention* is a thing—a learnable mental asset, with vast potential to change how you do your work and live your life.

In that book, Gallwey says focus of attention "is the quintessential component of superior performance in every activity." Managing focus is a master skill with unlimited application. He said the challenge is that you can't *force* your attention to stay at a single point, but you *can* relax your inner commentary so your attention can naturally settle on "critical variables," like the voice of a person who is with you.

KNOWING HOW TO DIRECT YOUR ATTENTION IS AN ESSENTIAL WORK AND LIFE SKILL

In the past decade, as work environments have been overwhelmed by the cacophony of email, Slack traffic, social media, and news streams, how we control our attention has become a hot topic within leadership and self-help circles. The term *attention* relates to how we notice or concentrate on some aspect of the vast field of information that surrounds us.

You can be more productive if you become more adept at concentrating your attention on your most important tasks, even if that requires ignoring lively distractions.

Beyond that, the way you choose to deploy your attention will shape how you see your life and everything around you. If you tend to dwell on the negative, the world seems dark. If you shift your focus to more positive elements in any situation, you will feel happier.

In Focus, *author Daniel Goleman describes "attention in all its varieties" as "an under-appreciated mental faculty." He says it shapes not only our awareness of the world but also the regulation of our thoughts and feelings.*

Goleman sorts the many aspects of attention into three kinds of focus:

1. *Inner focus* attunes us to our intuitions, values, and decisions.
2. *Other focus* is about our connections to other people.
3. *Outer focus* lets us navigate the larger world.

Our ability to focus our attention is not something that remains fixed. For example, if we stop serious reading and research after leaving school, we may find it more difficult to complete work projects that require concentrating deeply on a single challenge for an extended period.

Goleman suggests we think of attention as a mental muscle that we can strengthen by working out. He says meditation's "one-pointed focus" is one tool to strengthen our ability to tightly focus our attention.

EXERCISE:

To more consciously direct your attention at work, notice the length of time you are able to totally focus on a single task. From there, you might decide to lengthen the time you can stay focused.

To start the experiment, pick out a specific piece of challenging work and guess how long you'll be able to concentrate on it and nothing else. Say you need to draft a proposal and you estimate that you can concentrate for half an hour.

Clear your workspace and turn off notifications. Set a timer for thirty minutes and start working. Whenever you find yourself distracted, immediately turn back to your writing. Take a break when the alarm goes off.

If you can easily concentrate for the full thirty minutes, you may want to continue the experiment by trying longer work periods. If, however, you can't keep going for half an hour, you might want to build your ability to focus. Try the experiment for shorter time periods until you know how long you can concentrate exclusively on this one thing. From there, practice increasing your work blocks until you can focus your attention on one task for about twenty-five or thirty minutes.

Chapter 20

What Is Positivity and How Do You Get It?

There is a link between a positive attitude and career success. When we get bogged down in cynicism and negativity, our brains can get stuck in patterns that set us up for failure. If we can maintain a positive mindset, staying hopeful in even the worst of times, we are far more likely to become happier and more successful at work.

We've already explored many ways to feel more upbeat, and we'll touch on more as we go along. In this chapter I talk more about how I learned to fight off negativity. Plus, I share more from experts about the power of "positivity."

I LEARNED ABOUT BEING POSITIVE BY TRIAL AND ERROR, BUT YOU DON'T HAVE TO

Sometimes it takes me two steps to learn things that make a big difference in my life. First comes the epiphany: an "aha!" feeling arrives in a flash. Immediately, my view of the world shifts a bit. In the second step I spend a long time contemplating this new (to me) phenomenon, trying to understand how it works and why it took me so long to notice.

Earlier I described how the teenaged me stumbled on the concept of gradual change while staring at a spoonful of sugar. Seeing that heap of sugar helped me realize I could painlessly get over my craving for the sweet stuff by reducing it one grain at a time.

A bigger insight hit me when I was studying law. I was the classic struggling student, trying to keep up with my classes while paying my way through Georgetown Law. My stress was exacerbated by a fear that employers weren't yet ready to hire women lawyers. I felt sorry for myself and the world seemed dark.

Things got worse when I heard some bad news. During a routine exam, a doctor found an ugly mass on my brother's spine. Because of its location, if the tumor was malignant, it would be life threatening. My brother was rushed into surgery.

Happily, within hours I heard the news that the lump was benign.

My relief was intense. My dark mood suddenly disappeared. I felt lucky to be in school and confident I'd enjoy a wonderful career. In the following days I noticed that nothing had really changed in my life, and yet everything was different. My negative attitude had disappeared in an flash, and the world seemed full of opportunity.

I wasn't sure how it all worked, but I saw that much of my misery had been the result of my own negative attitude. So I decided to fight back the next time the pessimistic voice in my head started saying things like "I'll never find a job." I gradually learned to respond to that voice by replacing its downer messages with more positive self-talk.

Decades later, I'm a happy, optimistic person. Part of the change may simply be the result of getting older. In *The Happiness Curve*, Jonathan Rauch writes about the vast data suggesting that people gradually feel more satisfied with life after they move through middle age.

Researchers say our level of happiness tends to follow a "U" curve. Perhaps we are optimistic and ambitious in our twenties, but we start to feel disappointed with life as we age. Rauch said that in his forties he felt discontented and restless, like he'd wasted his life, even though he'd surpassed goals set in his twenties.

Eventually, the curve turns upward, and we feel happier again in our fifties. Rauch says it's not that the circumstances in your life get better; what changes is how you *feel* about your life. Recent research says if you are healthy, the rising curve may continue well into your eighties.

The reasons for the rebound in happiness after a midlife slump aren't clear. As I look around, I suspect two things often happen. Surviving the inevitable health challenges, career crises, and other losses actually makes us more aware of the good things in life. For example, after my husband recovered from cancer, we both experienced a new optimism and joy, a new kind of contentment that he labeled "the gift of cancer."

Also, through living life, we may learn that catastrophizing and berating ourselves are self-defeating. As we age, we gradually discover how to deal with tough times by facing the bad news, acknowledging our fear and sadness, then shifting our attention to the more positive aspects of our situation.

You don't have to wait until years of trial and error help you create a happier life and career. You can start right now by choosing positivity.

A major factor in my happiness is that early decision to more actively manage my attitude. I realized my response to challenges might depend less on the facts and more on how I felt about the facts. So I worked at becoming positive. You can do that too.

POSITIVE PSYCHOLOGISTS ARE TEACHING US TO BE MORE UPBEAT

In this section I mention a few books that helped me reject my natural pessimism and choose an upbeat frame of mind.

Almost twenty years ago I was fascinated when I started reading about a new breed of psychologists. Instead of focusing on ways to help mentally ill people get well, they were studying how to help well people feel even better. A book that grabbed my attention was *Learned Optimism* by Martin Seligman, often called "the father of Positive Psychology." His explanation of how we can choose to be happier in life reinforced my belief that we can *elect* to have a positive outlook.

Later I was captivated by Seligman's book *Flourish,* which describes how to build well-being, that state which is broader than happiness. In Seligman's view positive emotion is the cornerstone of well-being.

I also love *Positivity* by Barbara Fredrickson, a widely known expert on the topic. She describes positivity as a collection of positive emotions, the most common of which are joy, gratitude, serenity, interest, hope, pride, amusement, inspiration, awe, and love. Of these, one of the easiest to cultivate is gratitude.

In her book Fredrickson says that positivity "comes in many flavors." Whether you experience positivity "depends vitally on how you think. Positive emotions—like all emotions—arise from how you interpret events and ideas as they unfold."

Fredrickson suggests cultivating positivity offers tremendous advantages. It will broaden your outlook, allowing you to see more opportunities. It will unleash your creativity and innovation. And positivity "alters your brain and changes the way you interact with the world."

Positivity can produce "astonishingly disproportionate outcomes." Fredrickson says that "simply imagining a joyful memory or receiving a small kindness can make a difference in the ease with which people locate creative and optimal solutions to the problems they face on a daily basis."

Another favorite is *The Happiness Advantage* by Shawn Achor. He writes at length about how happy workers are more productive, are better leaders, and enjoy greater job security than their more negative peers.

Achor suggests you can build more happiness on the job by changing how you think about what you do. Having a negative view of your workplace can actually change the results of your efforts. If you think of your daily tasks as drudgery, they will become just that.

Just as your mindset about work affects your performance, your assessment of your ability will impact your success. Achor says, "Studies show that simply believing we can bring about positive change in our lives increases motivation and job performance; that success, in essence, becomes a self-fulfilling prophecy."

I'm not suggesting you need to read all these books. But I want you to know that if you are feeling skeptical about the power of a positive attitude, many interesting and readable books can help you understand how it works.

EXERCISE:

Start building your positivity habit by modifying your internal commentary. The goal is to start noticing and rejecting pessimistic thoughts.

Remind yourself for the next few days to remain alert to the grouchy part of your conscious self. Maybe you have an inner voice that repeats negative phrases, like "one more rotten day." Or perhaps you hear yourself complaining out loud. Consider listing or journaling about those whiney comments, whether they pop into your head or reach the tip of your tongue.

Just becoming aware of your negative patterns can help you move past them. The next step is to fight back. Once you identify a recurring complaint or grumpy prediction, practice letting it float out of your head, and replace it with a more positive statement. You can argue with your whiney thought pattern like you would with an annoying friend.

Chapter 21

Feel Better by Doing Something Kind

Feeling more positive can trigger an upward spiral of productivity and success on the job. Shifting negative thought patterns is one effective way to become more upbeat. *However, the fastest route to feeling happier is to* do *something.*

Taking action can spark a surge of positivity, and the first step doesn't have to be big. In college, when I was in despair about the limited opportunities for women, I started doing my "sugar grains." Every day I'd do a little something, perhaps as small as offering encouragement to another woman. As I became more brave, my acts became more bold. But the shift in my mood happened the instant I adopted my sugar grain *plan* and did the first little thing.

Doing something—and having a firm plan to do more later—brings satisfaction, hope for the future, and new energy.

Sometimes when I push myself to act, I do things so tiny they're just a hair bigger than a thought. One such action might be described as "sending a blessing." Perhaps across the room in a meeting, I spot a woman I know is facing a tough time. Or staring through a bus window, I spot an old guy slipping and falling on the ice. I feel bad for these folks, but I'm not in a position to offer assistance.

So I try to send them loving energy. I imagine a spiral of red light flowing from my heart to theirs. All I am "doing" is feeling love and visualizing a way to pass it along. I can't claim that my ray of light actually hits the target. But it does make me feel more aware of other people and perhaps more alert to opportunities for kindness. It feels like I've done something and encourages me to do more.

YOUR KIND ACT CAN
MAKE YOU FEEL GOOD

A powerful way to initiate positivity is to *do something kind* that actually helps another person. Behaving in a kind way has a measurable impact on your health and happiness. *In* **Flourish,** *Martin Seligman says, "Scientists have found that doing a kindness produces the single most reliable momentary increase in well-being of any exercise we have tested."*

Your brain responds positively when you are cooperative, generous, or helpful to another person. The warm glow you get from your kind gesture is associated with a sense of connection. Because cooperation was a life-and-death matter when our hunter/gatherer ancestors worked together to find enough food, we evolved to feel better when we feel connected.

One small kindness might generate a positive loop. Say the person in front of you in the coffee line drops her umbrella. You pick it up and hand it to her. She smiles and thanks you. You smile back and chat for a minute. Here's what happens: you feel good about being helpful, and then you feel even better when you exchange words and smiles. From there, each of you might smile at another person, broadening the loop.

In **Positivity,** *Barbara Fredrickson says that kindness and positivity feed on each other.* You can further increase your positivity by stepping up the cadence and size of your kind actions. She recommends not only maintaining your typical expressions of kindness on normal days but also creating "kindness days," for helping friends or nonprofit groups.

How much of a boost you get from your kind or generous act may depend on your attitude. If you help somebody just because you think you must, your good deed may not feel satisfying. If you are motivated by a sense of joy or purpose, your kindness will cause your energy to spike.

EXERCISE:

Schedule a "kindness day" and commit yourself to doing at least five kind things. The kind acts you can perform in a single day are endless, but here are some suggestions:

1. Offer to help a struggling colleague.

2. Go to a crowdfunding website like GoFundMe, browse through the categories of fundraisers, and make a donation.

3. Contact friends you haven't seen in a while and let them know you miss them.

4. Write a LinkedIn recommendation.

5. Thank someone who has made a difference in your career.

6. Leave a large tip for a harassed-looking server.

7. At an event, introduce yourself to a stranger who looks lonely.

8. Offer authentic praise to a person who has done good work.

9. If you're faced with a decision that would impact another person, first ask yourself: "What would kindness do?"

Chapter 22

Build Positivity by Creating Rituals

A ritual is a carefully defined, meaningful routine you perform regularly. You may do it every day, but it's not the same as a habit because it's not automatic—you have to think about it. You regularly *choose* to do it, perhaps because it clarifies your intention, shapes your mood, or keeps you grounded.

Rituals work best when you act mindfully, going through steps that bring you fully to the present. Some rituals, like daily meditation or prayer, can be a way of giving thanks and acknowledging your values. Productivity rituals like identifying your most important task of the day can help you stay on track. Social rituals like a monthly team lunch or family game night can help people remain connected.

SHARED RITUALS CAN ENRICH YOUR LIFE, LIKE THIS DOES FOR ME

Near the end of 2008, my journalist husband, Andy Alexander, was offered a two-year term as ombudsman for the *Washington Post*. Recognizing the importance of this challenge, Andy left his job as Washington bureau chief for Cox Newspapers and moved to the *Post*.

Andy's role as ombudsman was to be "the readers' representative and an internal critic of *Washington Post* journalism." His job was to "watch over" the *Post*'s journalistic integrity and act as an advocate for readers. At that time, the newspaper industry was entering its years of crisis, and all news media were caught up in rapid change. Newspaper readers—always a scrappy bunch—were angry and had plenty of grievances.

In his new role, Andy worked long hours, answering thousands of calls and emails from readers, investigating their complaints, and keeping a close eye on the newsroom. The pressure would increase as the week wore on because Andy's high-profile Sunday column was due to the editor on Friday night. He had a few hours of downtime on Saturday, but that ended in the evening when his column appeared online, stimulating a new flood of email. His workweek started again by early Sunday morning.

After a few weeks it was clear that the intensity of this new schedule wouldn't be good for Andy's health or our marriage. So we created a new ritual: every Saturday *without fail* we would go out to lunch together. Sometimes we discussed a bit of business, like household questions or scheduling. But we always dealt with logistical matters quickly and approached every lunch as a fun, relaxing date where we could focus on each other.

During Andy's ombudsman years, our Saturday lunch helped us feel that all was well. We always could count on some time together soon, so we never felt too out of touch. Now our lives are more relaxed, but our lunch ritual remains a fundamental part of our schedule.

PRODUCTIVITY RITUALS CAN HELP YOU FEEL MORE IN CONTROL OF YOUR WORK

If you want to experiment with rituals that might help you find more satisfaction in your job, consider a routine to get each day off to a good start. Morning rituals are highly individual but could include elements like these:

1. **Exercise.** You might feel more energetic if your day begins with at least ten minutes of yoga or stretching, or a quick walk or run.

2. **Meditation.** A mindfulness practice is a good way to start each day in a positive mood and with an enhanced ability to focus.

3. **"Big Three" list.** Create a foundation for success by pausing each morning to identify your top three priorities for the day. Remind yourself *why* they matter and *how* you will organize yourself to make progress.

4. **Gratitude exercise.** Make a list, write a thank-you note, pray, or choose another way to focus on the good things in your life and the best parts of your work. It takes just a couple of minutes to lift your mood.

5. **Journal.** Writing even a short entry can build your self-awareness and help put your day in perspective.

EXERCISE:

Create a morning ritual. Ask yourself how you would like to change your typical day. Do you want to be more organized? Less stressed? In a better mood? Identify at least one area where you want improvement and design a new morning routine that could help. Stick with it for at least two weeks; then assess your experience and decide whether to continue this ritual or try another approach.

Chapter 23

See Things More Clearly by Mapping the Big Picture

During a coaching session my client may be wrestling with a broad question like "How do I get a promotion?" When you're grappling with a major job challenge, you can easily feel daunted by a confusing mass of factors. The lingering uncertainty can leave you stuck or unhappy for months.

A complex question or challenge becomes more manageable if you can step back and see the bigger picture. *For some people the perfect way to scope out a complicated dilemma or opportunity is to create a mind map.*

A mind map is a branching diagram used to describe a concept, project, or situation. As the illustration on the next page suggests, each map is structured roughly like a wheel. The hub is an icon that represents the theme you want to explore. The branches flowing directly from the hub represent the main elements of your topic. Those branches are further divided into subtopics, with the process continuing for as long as you have room.

Mind maps can be a helpful way to organize and sort out information. I sometimes use them for taking meeting notes, including when I'm getting to know a new client. Within working groups, mapping can help team members develop a shared vision of their goals and responsibilities.

Fans of mapping say the process encourages analysis and planning in a way that reflects how our brains make associations. Maps move us from the trap of linear thinking, encouraging us to become more creative. As our map evolves, we might spot

This mind map uses my career as a simplified example.

connections or new directions that we would otherwise have missed. Beyond that, the visual nature of maps is said to stimulate the creative part of our brains.

One thing I like about a good map is that a single glance allows you to recall a complete, complicated picture. The image of a map becomes more memorable than hundreds of descriptive words. Many mappers believe that their most effective diagrams feature colors, arrows, and cartoons that grab attention and instantly trigger a memory or impression.

For me, mapping feels more fluid if I do it by hand. Others prefer software that makes it easy to revise and manage large amounts of data. For business activities I sometimes use FreeMind, a free mapping application you can download from Wikipedia.

A mind map can help you gain perspective on just about any problem. Once you can see the big picture and spot starting points for moving forward, the issue may feel more manageable. And you may feel more positive.

THESE GUIDELINES CAN HELP
YOU DRAW A MIND MAP

Before beginning a map, be clear about exactly what you want to explore. In just a few words describe the single goal, situation, or problem you propose to examine. Select an image, word, or initial to represent your central theme and place it in the middle of your page.

From that center, draw branches representing major thoughts or categories related to your central theme. Expand on your main thoughts with smaller branches representing sub-ideas.

These tips will help you create a vivid map:

1. **Be brief.** Try to use only one word to label each branch. A single-word label not only saves space but also seems most effective at capturing ideas and triggering connections.

2. **Create icons.** A picture can be worth a thousand words, and imagery is a powerful component of mapping. Simple pictures can symbolize multifaceted situations. Consider how a religious icon—like a cross or crescent and star—might remind you of deep values and experiences.

3. **Color code.** Use colors or shapes to represent moods or categories of ideas.

4. **Connect.** Use arrows, dotted lines, or background shading to show relationships among various categories.

5. **Work quickly.** To start, draw swiftly and don't worry about perfection. Don't bother to edit or make judgments about your work. You'll have time for refinements later, but a quick start might help you make connections and spot relationships that you haven't considered.

6. **Have fun.** Don't be afraid to be silly while creating your map. A benefit of mapping is that it can help you break out of your same old ways of thinking. If you play with cartoons or invent emojis, thinking outside the box might be easier.

EXERCISE:

Create a map of your career, either the one you have now or the one you want.

The illustration on page 90 is a simplified version of the map I drew years ago, when I left my corporate job and launched a portfolio of work activities. The image still reminds me that my career includes both paid and nonprofit work. The fitness branch is a reminder that I can't do my best work if I'm not in shape.

Career mapping can be helpful whether you're feeling unhappy with your job or eager to make it even more interesting. If you are wondering how to juggle career and life goals, your map may bring new insights. Don't worry if you don't know everything you want. Go ahead and map what you *do* know.

1. **Start** in the center of the page with an icon or initial that represents you.

2. **Draw major branches and sub-branches** and label them to represent key elements of your work life, like your mission and values, tasks or lines of business, financial security, skills and expertise, network, schedule, or self-improvement goals.

3. **Decorate** the map and provide richer detail using pictures, colors, boxes, or different types of text. Images can be powerful. (One client kept herself on track by creating a charm bracelet with each charm representing a major element on the map of her ideal life.)

4. **Humor** can make your map more vivid and easier to recall.

Chapter 24

How to Get Moving When You Don't Feel Motivated

On a gray January day in Washington, I spoke with a string of clients suffering from the blahs. The wintry mood seemed to hit even Larry, a young sales manager who normally brims with enthusiasm. When we met for lunch, he seemed determined to stay miserable for a while.

Larry said that recently he had totally lost his motivation at work. He complained that January is normally slow in his industry, but this year things were worse than usual because his boss wasn't doing anything to generate opportunities.

"How can I get myself motivated about work?" he asked.

I asked about what he had tried and techniques he might explore, but he dismissed every possibility. Finally, I shrugged my shoulders and said, "I can suggest options, but I can't make you feel motivated if you're not willing to try."

Larry sounded half amused and half serious when he asked, "What happened to your compassion? At least when I talk with my wife and my mother, they sympathize with me. But all you want to do is kick me in the butt."

"You're right," I said. "You say you want to be more motivated, so I'm talking to you exactly like I sometimes talk to myself."

One option for Larry was to not worry about his short-term lack of motivation. Sometimes it's fine to take a little time off and shift your attention to other things, like your fitness program, your social life, or an outside interest. Relaxing your obsession with work gives your brain a chance to process months of input and can be a good way to generate fresh ideas and a more upbeat attitude.

Larry said, "I don't need a break because I had a long vacation last month. And I *want* to be motivated. It feels terrible to come to work and not accomplish anything."

Larry needed to stop complaining and *do* something. Instead of wallowing in negativity, waiting for motivation to hit, *he needed to take action.*

Motivation is an urge that builds when you accomplish things. Motivation often follows action, not the other way around.

Like I told Larry, if you're in the dumps, it's time to identify a task you'd do today if only you felt motivated. Next, immediately start *doing* that task. If it's too big to complete in one sitting, break it into small pieces you can complete in an hour. The good feelings following each completed piece will stimulate you to tackle the next one. *Finishing your series of tasks will help you generate more enthusiasm about your next project.*

Larry identified a few tasks to speed through, and his success in knocking them off his "to-do" list made him feel more energetic. Next, he spent an hour writing brief descriptions of three potential projects for the coming year. He invited his team to explore possibilities. They liked two options and everyone started working on proposals for Larry's boss.

As soon as things got busy, Larry forgot about his lack of motivation.

HERE ARE MORE WAYS TO MOTIVATE YOURSELF AT WORK

1. **Revisit the Engagement Triangle.** Remind yourself *why* you are doing this work and how your achievement will impact your future. Focus on the three keys to happiness at

work: your purpose, the people around you, and the satisfaction that comes from managing your performance.

2. **Remind yourself of your values.** Write for a few minutes about the kind of professional you want to be. Are you committed to a set of professional standards? Are you inspired by certain principles, like "Do my best every day"?

3. **Let go of negative emotions.** Sometimes your lack of motivation isn't caused by your work, so much as by unhappiness about life in general. You can lift your mood with some of the techniques discussed so far, like writing about the good stuff, meditating, or taking a walk. When you feel more positive, it's easier to spot opportunities and become excited about projects.

4. **Make yourself accountable to others.** Identify a project that will involve working with other people toward a deadline. Schedule an event, collaborate on an article, or offer to present a report at an upcoming meeting. Your commitment to collaborators will drive you to action.

5. **Challenge your excuses.** When I spoke with Larry, he had excuses suggesting that nothing could get him out of his funk. It was too cold to take an invigorating walk. He couldn't plan anything because he didn't know his boss's goals. When you hear yourself making excuses instead of plans, it's time to fight back. Write down every excuse that pops into your head, and for each one make a plan to move forward anyway.

— KEY TAKEAWAY —

Self-motivation isn't something you just happen
to have. It's an internal drive that you can build when
you want to.

If you feel unmotivated, remind yourself why your
work matters. Acknowledge your capacity to grow, and
identify skills and values that brought you to this point.
Generate momentum *right now* by working intensely on
a task you can complete in less than an hour.

Recall the feedback loop: motivation drives you
to action, and action makes you feel motivated.
When you're bogged down, it's time to act.

Chapter 25

Your Calendar Is More than a Meeting List

Greeting each morning with a positive mindset is not enough. In a hectic world, resolutions to have a good, productive day can fall apart if you don't consciously allocate your time, energy, and attention.

Making each day more rewarding often starts by taking control of your time. A starting point is selecting a calendar that works for you. The choices feel endless. Some professionals are tied to software that links them to colleagues' schedules and collective workflows. Others manage their projects, and their whole lives, with bullet journals or elaborate hardbound planning calendars.

What matters is not the format of your calendar but how you use it to plan each day and make the most of the minutes that are within your control.

You can create a more fulfilling work life if you schedule as much as possible, then check your calendar frequently, and stick with your commitments. You'll feel less anxious and more in charge when you are sure you're not missing key deadlines or appointments. If you build the habit of *relying* on your calendar, you're more likely to keep moving even when you aren't feeling motivated.

EXAMINE WHERE YOUR TIME GOES

Do you sometimes feel that you lose track of time? Even if top tasks and events show up on your calendar, some days you ignore them and time passes in a blur. In the evening you realize you're exhausted but made no progress on your highest priorities.

If you're not accomplishing enough with your available time, a useful exercise is to track all your activities for at least one week. Good data will give you a better understanding of your challenges and activity patterns.

One tracking approach is to create a spreadsheet for the work-week and note what you do in each hour-long block. Or you might make notes about your activities directly onto your calendar. Apps like RescueTime can help create detailed records of how you spend your days.

However you record your activities, you may be surprised when you see where some of your minutes actually go. When you study your time logs, you may realize you've given away too many minutes. Perhaps you've been accepting all meeting invitations without saving hours for your top priorities. Or you're devoting a big chunk of the day to answering messages that feel urgent but aren't really that important.

INCREASE THE VALUE OF YOUR CALENDAR AS A PLANNING TOOL

You're likely to get more done if you use your calendar to help sort your priorities as you plan your available time. These scheduling techniques can help you make better use of the minutes you control:

1. **Plan ahead.** You probably book meetings on your calendar weeks in advance. You should do the same thing with your highest priority work. If you have a critical project deadline in two weeks, pause right now to put time blocks on your calendar for working on that project between now and the due date.

2. **Plan each week.** Create a habit of looking ahead as each new week begins. Think about how a successful week

would look. Review your priorities, create a short list of your top tasks, and make sure there is time for them on your calendar.

3. **Plan each day in detail.** Each morning, visualize how you want the day to go and confirm the important details on your calendar. Make sure you have space for your top three goals for the day. Schedule as much of your activity as possible, including your breaks.

4. **Fight back on meeting creep.** If you have so many meetings you can't get anything done, look for ways to push back. Start by excusing yourself from meetings where you're not needed. Delay appointments that have value but aren't urgent. Send someone else if you have the power to delegate. Plan shorter events, so if a regular meeting takes an hour, suggest restructuring it to last forty-five minutes.

5. **Set alerts.** Use your calendar notification system, ask Alexa, or choose other tools to remind yourself to stick to your schedule. Warn yourself not only when it's time for a meeting, but also when you should start a block of project time. When you begin activities that can be time sucks, like email or social media, set a timer to tell you when to quit.

6. **Limit multitasking.** A few people still brag about their ability to do several things at once. *But the research is clear: multitasking zaps productivity.* When you juggle two tasks, about 20 percent of your time is lost in switching back and forth. If you're handling a slew of things at once, you can lose more than half of your productive minutes. One way to reduce jumping between tools and tasks is to batch similar activities together. That might mean setting aside thirty minutes for all your quick calls and messages or completing several Excel tasks in the same time block.

— KEY TAKEAWAY —

A detailed calendar can be your friend, guiding
you throughout the day, helping you stay calm,
maximizing your control, and reminding you
to restore your energy by taking breaks.

Chapter 26

Your Calendar Should Reflect Both Your Priorities and Your Energy

Maintaining a detailed calendar and checking it often to be sure you're on track can make work feel more satisfying and successful. Feeling confident that the important things are indeed on your schedule can ease your worry.

PRIORITIZE YOUR ACTIVITIES

When you have more things to do than you can possibly accomplish, make sure your calendar does have room for your top priorities. Many tasks may feel pressing but as you continue to allocate your time, keep asking yourself: is this activity important enough to use time that could go to a key project?

If you keep refocusing on the things that matter most, you are more likely to move them forward. *One tool to help clarify which tasks deserve prime calendar spots is the Engagement Triangle. It can help you make good choices by reminding you of your guiding purpose, important human relationships, and rewarding ways to approach work.*

As you weigh the importance of various activities, ask yourself questions like these:

1. Purpose:
   - Does this activity support the organization's goals? My team's mission? My personal values?

- Is it specifically mentioned in my job description? My contract? My current assignments?
- How will the results influence the success of my job?
- How might this activity support my long-term objectives?

2. People:

- Will my results affect my colleagues' ability to do their jobs?
- Who are the "customers" for this work? Who else will be impacted?
- Will my boss's success be affected by my achievement?
- Does this activity bring opportunities to build relationships?

3. Performance:

- What kind of professional do I want to be, and how might I apply those standards here?
- How do I want other people to evaluate my work?
- How might I approach this challenge so that it helps me grow and learn?
- Is this a task where perfection isn't required and "good enough" will meet the need?

Once you are clear about which tasks are most important, don't delay allocating time for them on your schedule. When a key project seems too big to schedule, identify small tasks that will help move it forward. Find time slots for those little actions, even when it means renegotiating other commitments.

CONSIDER YOUR ENERGY PATTERNS AS YOU SCHEDULE YOUR WORK

You can be more productive by tackling your top priorities in blocks of time when your energy is most likely to be high.

Think of your energy level as a measure of your capacity to work and enjoy life. Your energy naturally ebbs and flows, partly because it's tied to daily rhythms (known as "circadian" rhythms). In other words, you likely have more get-up-and-go at some times of day than at others.

Body rhythms vary from person to person, but many feel sharpest in the morning and experience a slump after lunch. Others are night owls, and their juices don't truly start flowing until later in the day.

You're more likely to maximize your cognitive and other abilities if you consider your body clock when you plan your day. If you know you're typically most alert in the morning, don't waste those precious early hours on low-value work, like answering routine email. Devote your peak hours to work that matters most.

As you schedule, keep in mind that humans achieve more by doing sprints, not marathons. You can't keep doing the same thing for long periods and continue to produce top-level work. It's not physically possible. Most people can push hard on a single task for only about thirty to ninety minutes; then their pace slows and the quality of their work suffers. It's time for a rest.

Because of the way your body and brain go through short cycles, organize your workflow into manageable segments, usually no more than an hour long, interrupted by breaks or changes in pace.

One benefit of scheduling your work in segments is it allows you to recover from periods of intense work and build new energy for your next burst of accomplishment. *Let's emphasize this: unlike time, which is limited, fresh energy can be generated. Your capacity for intense work can be restored, and careful scheduling can help.*

Throughout this book we explore ways to build *positivity.* That term means not only promoting positive emotions but also generating positive physical, mental, and spiritual energy. *You can renew your energy level in the course of your workday in many ways, such as:*

- Putting aside dull tasks to spend half an hour on your favorite project
- Meditating for a few minutes
- Taking a quick walk, preferably outdoors
- Connecting with a person you like
- Taking a short nap
- Standing and stretching

TO MAXIMIZE ENERGY, STAND UP!

Not only is walking great for your well-being, it also provides terrific thinking time. When you're stuck on a problem or searching for inspiration, try leaving your workspace and taking a walk. The exercise stimulates regions of your brain not triggered by conscious, analytical thinking, and might spark a burst of creativity, bringing you a breakthrough.

Taking a half-hour walk can help you feel alert and at the top of your game. But one daily walk isn't enough. You'll be sharper and more energetic if you also frequently get out of your chair and stand for a while.

Human bodies aren't designed for long hours of sitting. In *Sitting Kills, Moving Heals*, former NASA health sciences director Joan Vernikos explains that our bodies were designed to engage in perpetual motion. When studying how to keep astronauts healthy in space, Vernikos and her NASA colleagues discovered that good health requires continuous, low-intensity movement that challenges the force of gravity.

After you sit for thirty minutes, your metabolism slows down, leg and other muscles shut off, your back can start hurting, and systems throughout the body function less efficiently. You may start to feel sluggish. And sitting for long periods can lead to heart disease, cancer, depression, and obesity.

Some doctors say that sitting for more than eight hours a day is worse for you than smoking. Recommendations on how often you should stand vary, but many experts suggest you stand and stretch *at least* once every hour.

— KEY TAKEAWAY —

Planning your day requires more than arbitrarily assigning spaces on your calendar. Start by thinking about your top priorities and consider the activities that will move them forward. Identify time slots when you're most likely to feel energetic, and save them for the most demanding of your tasks.

Keep your energy flowing by organizing your work into thirty- to ninety-minute blocks, broken up by breaks. Vary your activities so you're not doing the same kind of work for too long. Stand up regularly throughout each day.

Chapter 27

Align Your Priorities
with Your Attention

You are likely to be more fully engaged in your work if you remain aware of how you direct your attention. Staring at a screen may feel like you're working, but you're not accomplishing much if your mind is off somewhere else, like eavesdropping on a colleague or planning lunch.

Where you focus your attention helps shape the quality of your day. Regularly being reminded of your top priorities makes it easier to ignore random information and remain alert to developments that impact your key objectives.

Productivity expert Maura Nevel Thomas* teaches professionals to regain control over their lives and work by managing their attention. She says, "Attention management is the most essential skill you need to live a life of choice rather than a life of reaction and distraction."

Thomas says managing your attention is more challenging these days because distractions are everywhere in our technology-rich, always-on environment. She says a starting point for regaining control is to notice the habitual ways your attention tends to wander. That requires spotting cues that prompt you to shift your focus, like message notifications or social media alerts.

The ability to direct your attention can make a tremendous difference in the quality of your work. In *Deep Work*, Georgetown University professor Cal Newport describes the kinds of challenging tasks that demand your *full* attention. Deep work might involve any kind of pursuit that requires a high level of skill and has the power to give you a sense of satisfaction.

You have to concentrate intensely to do deep work, and that isn't always easy. Most people can't plunge into work quickly because it takes a moment to focus completely and start digging into a project.

The effort is worthwhile. *Deep work brings you insights, translates into progress on key projects, and helps you grow.*

Concentrating deeply allows you to optimize your performance and sometimes to achieve the wonderful sense of flow that comes when all your resources are fully engaged.

Thomas says you can't *force* yourself to harness your attention and concentrate intensely. Instead, she suggests you schedule deep work at the times when you have the best chance of feeling mindful and focused. This might mean finding times when you can turn off all distractions, center yourself with a few deep breaths, then commit to working on a single project for at least an hour.

Other kinds of work don't require such an intense focus. In hours when your environment is hectic or your energy is low, schedule tasks that are more compatible with frequent interruptions. I like to group similar, undemanding tasks—like answering routine email—for the times when I'm not at my best. I try to save the quieter, less distracting times for writing and other projects where I need to stay focused.

— KEY TAKEAWAY —

To get the full value of your calendar, it's important to schedule top-priority tasks at the times you can best focus your attention. As you allocate time slots, identify good windows for concentrating on deep work. Schedule lower-priority activity for times when it's more difficult to concentrate or you are forced to multitask.

Chapter 28

Learning Helps You Enjoy Work, Keep Growing, and Find Opportunities

We've talked about why to vary your blocks of work time—and build in breaks—as you plan each day. You're more effective when you oscillate between activities, shifting from deep work to multitasking, from pushing yourself to resting. It's difficult to maintain a steady grind for hours at a time without losing efficiency. Occasionally changing gears makes concentrating easier, and your creativity and awareness are refreshed.

Another consideration when you're laying out the day's plan is how to schedule learning activities. Any day feels more rewarding if it includes intervals to stretch your mind and concentrate on something new.

In *The Power of Mindful Learning,* psychologist Ellen Langer says that finding a way to learn something new always makes work feel more like play. She says what makes a puzzle or game enjoyable is "the process of going from not knowing to knowing." And it can be the same on the job.

Going further, Langer says work is more fun if we can focus on the nuances and find ways to deepen our understanding. Virtually any job offers more freedom to notice distinctions and possibilities than might first appear. Langer suggests finding them can be a matter of adopting a positive attitude and putting your mind to it. The more deeply you engage in a task, the more you'll learn and the more quickly time will speed by.

Part of the excitement that comes from learning is the thrill of satisfaction when you find each new thing. To our brains, acquiring a bit of understanding feels like a success. As we continue to make progress, small insights are rewarded with hits of dopamine.

Aside from making work more fun, committing yourself to continuing learning can bring tremendous career benefits. Here are three more reasons to make learning activities a high priority in your career:

1. **To remain relevant.** In a fast-paced world, no profession remains the same for long. Even if you're at the top of your game now, your skills will become outdated if you don't keep up with your field. The threat of obsolescence is just one side of the coin. On the other is the good news: your opportunities will increase as you expand your expertise and extend your ability to dive into challenging questions.

2. **To become more resilient.** People who approach work in a spirit of learning may find it much easier to deal effectively with failed efforts. Avid learners tend to see the big picture and focus on the whole process. When the unexpected happens, they are able to step back, assess the situation, and quickly consider next steps.

3. **To be authentic and centered.** There's a sort of chicken-and-egg loop between learning and positivity. When you're truly involved in learning, you're being totally yourself. You forget about what others think and keep diving further into the effort. In *Never Stop Learning,* Professor Bradley Staats suggests that as you keep going, you trigger a rewarding sense of mastery, autonomy, and purpose. As you focus more completely, the authenticity of your effort

triggers positive emotions, which motivate you to learn even more.

THERE ARE MANY WAYS TO INJECT MORE LEARNING INTO YOUR JOB

If you contemplate your calendar, your work habits, and the people you know, you're likely to spot opportunities to build more learning into many days. *These suggestions can help make learning a bigger part of your job:*

1. **Keep a learning list.** When you catch yourself thinking "that sounds interesting" or "I wish I knew more," make a note. Always maintain a list of possible learning topics, and create study plans for when you have a few free minutes.

2. **Try micro-learning.** Building knowledge in tiny steps has been around for a long time. I recall word-of-the-day desk calendars and foreign language flashcards from my childhood. Now there are endless options for ordering up bite-size content. Depending on your field, you can find TED Talks that are right on target, free courses featuring five-minute modules, daily newsletters, and apps that feature games to help you build skill.

3. **Get more from your daily activities.** Often we attend meetings and join calls without fully tuning in to what's going on. *Almost everywhere you go, there's an opportunity to learn if you decide to focus.* One habit of constant learners is mindful engagement, which means paying attention to whatever is going on right now.

4. **Listen and ask.** Learn more by rejecting the assumption that you know everything about anything. Remind yourself that there's *always* a good chance of additional information. In meetings this might mean forcing yourself to listen carefully, even if your kneejerk reaction is "this is

boring." Find times to ask others for a different perspective and listen without judgment to what they have to say.

5. **Teach.** A terrific way to master a topic is to teach it to somebody else. You don't need to have the expertise when you start. If a new technology is interesting, or an emerging trend seems relevant to your team's work, volunteer to learn about it and then report back to the group.

6. **Interact with well-informed people.** Open minds can be contagious. A good way to become a stronger learner is to regularly spend time with broadly educated, intellectually curious people.

7. **Be a specialist *and* a generalist.** Constant learning is necessary for keeping your professional skills up to date. But Professor Staats says that, while it's important to keep growing your specialized expertise, a thriving career requires more. *In a world where everything is connected and innovation jumps from industry to industry, the savviest learners also pursue variety.* They keep looking for interesting new developments, and they are as willing to study fresh topics as humble beginners.

8. **Schedule time for deep learning.** Some pursuits are well suited to gradual micro-learning, but complicated topics require lengthier dedicated time blocks. Analyzing new developments in your area of expertise or studying emerging trends may require you to focus on the material, read with care, ponder, and probably make notes. Deep learning involves a commitment, starting with finding time on your calendar.

9. **Get smarter.** We humans are good at building skills and expanding our abilities. *Just like building your muscles, you can improve your cognitive functioning and build a stronger brain.* You can increase your intelligence by challenging

yourself with difficult reading or demanding new activities. You can expand your capacity to do good work by pursuing stretch goals. Even if you don't feel talented, you can increase your skill at just about anything by *practicing* it, frequently and mindfully.

— KEY TAKEAWAY —

Continuous learning is vital to a satisfying career. Acquiring knowledge and competencies to expand your skill set is a good way to attract an interesting flow of opportunities.

Beyond keeping you relevant in your current field, continuous learning will help you understand the broader world and prepare for the unexpected. Being knowledgeable will broaden your range of future options and help you innovate in the job you have now.

Most important, learning is fun. It can transfer routine work into a continuing adventure. And constant learners tend to be interesting to other people.

Chapter 29

A Smart Path to Career Growth: Read More Books

I'm guessing you love books. Having a passion for reading books can help you learn, make you happier, and stimulate your career.

Reading is a skill you have to acquire and keep practicing, not an innate ability like speech. Whether you prefer reading online or on paper, developing the skill brings many benefits and enhances job skills. *Keeping up your reading can expand your base of knowledge, improve your intelligence and memory, stimulate creativity, help you become a better writer, and broaden your career options.*

Some kinds of reading, like fiction and memoirs, cause you to visualize scenes where the characters are interacting. This can help you develop empathy and an understanding of a wider range of people. Reading can be good for you when it's fun and relaxing because it helps you feel connected while giving you a break from real life.

Reading helps keep you sharp, and research says there's something special about reading **books.** For one thing, neuroscience suggests it's good for your brain. When you peruse books, as opposed to shorter articles, you're more likely to engage in "deep reading." That's a slow, immersive process, where you think about the content, pause, and perhaps reread a sentence and see connections with other topics.

Apparently, deep reading gives your brain a robust workout, energizing multiple cognitive functions. The brain engagement in reading books may be so healthy that it can even help you live longer. One National Institutes of Health study found that those who read books live longer than nonreaders or those who read only periodicals.

Reading a physical book may have a more profound impact than reading the same words on a tablet. That's because e-books lack "spatial navigability" and don't provide tangible cues, like the number of pages left in a volume. The different impact may be greater for readers—like me—who engage even more actively with our physical books. If I own a helpful book, I underline or highlight passages, mark pages with tabs, and write copious notes in the margins.

Any mode of reading is usually a more profound experience than listening to the audio version of the same book. Reading is something you *do*, while listening is less active. With audio, it's more difficult to pause and consider a sentence. The reader keeps talking, even when your mind wanders.

SERIOUS READING HELPS CREATE CAREER RESILIENCE

Centuries before science explained why reading is so good for your brain, leaders and teachers began describing it as vital to happiness and success.

Reading allows you to borrow knowledge from today's innovators as well as from wise people in distant times and places. You don't have to learn everything on your own, by trial and error.

Benjamin Franklin attributed much of his professional satisfaction and success to his reading and writing skills. He was self-educated and said he became a writer by studying books, often late into the night.

In his autobiography, Franklin said his "first project of a public nature" was the creation of a subscription library in Philadelphia. He called it "the mother of all North American subscription libraries. . . . These libraries have improved the general conversation of the Americans, made the common tradesmen and farmers as intelligent as most gentlemen from other countries."

Widespread literacy is woven into the American Dream, where success is possible for all who are willing to study and work. My prediction is that the skill of deep reading will be a key to career resilience in the hectic years to come.

The workplace is changing so rapidly that it's hard to predict which occupations will be thriving in future decades. While some positions are disappearing, employers are begging for applicants with new skill sets needed right now.

Part of being happy in your career is feeling confident that you can find a job in the future, regardless of what happens with your current gig. Another essential is professional flexibility, so you know change is always possible and new opportunities will appear if the old ones become unrewarding.

If you keep up your reading skills, you will always have the power to expand or completely reinvent your professional profile. If you are twenty-five today, you could easily work for another fifty years. Perhaps you'll change careers many times. If you know how to *learn*, the possibilities for growth and variety will be endless.

If you are sixty today and still building your learning ability, you have career potential that was unimaginable when you were twenty-five.

— KEY TAKEAWAY —

Reading, particularly reading books, can make you healthier and happier. If you keep building your reading skills, you will always have the ability to learn new things and reinvent a work life that serves you well.

Chapter 30

Improve Your Writing to Boost Your Performance

If you're thinking about creating a learning plan at work, here's a suggestion: devote time and energy to becoming a better writer. An ability to write serves you well in any job.

Writing is often the best way to organize your thoughts and share them with somebody else. Well-written messages let you describe what you know, want, and need.

Careful writing allows you to keep good records and shine a light on your achievements. If you write with clarity, you can always polish your brand, promote your skills and products, and present yourself to the broader world.

If writing in a work context is not one of your strengths, improving your writing skill has the potential to boost your career. If you're already a decent writer, polishing your skill can help you become more respected and influential.

SHARPEN YOUR WRITING TO EMPOWER YOUR CAREER

Carla Bass*, author of *Write to Influence!*, helps people boost their careers by becoming better business writers. In our podcast conversation, Bass explained how her passion for powerful writing dates back to her years as a colonel in the US Air Force.

When she was stationed in Hawaii, Bass was assigned to take over leadership of a squadron with a reputation for below-average work. As she became acquainted with her new team of 480 men and women, Bass found them to be talented and good at their jobs. She was puzzled by why such strong workers had such a bad rep, so she did a little detective work.

After going through masses of records, Bass concluded that the unit had received years of bad marks from superior officers because the squadron supervisors were doing a terrible job of reporting on achievements. Airmen were often doing excellent work but didn't get the credit because the bosses couldn't tell their story.

Bass decided the starting point for improving the unit's standing was to teach its supervisors how to write routine reports. She put together a handbook of writing tips (the first version of her excellent guidebook) and started teaching her troops. She said they gradually began to sweep the performance rewards, and her unit became the squadron to beat.

During her next fifteen years, Bass taught thousands of people throughout the Air Force. Since her retirement she has continued to teach powerful writing to government officials, business executives, and ambassadors.

Bass says the trick to life-changing writing is to make each word and every second of the reader's time play to your advantage. Here are a few of her writing tips :

1. **Proofread.** Check everything you write to be sure you've covered the basics, like proper punctuation and spelling,

2. **Be clear.** Write simple, succinct sentences, and avoid bureaucratic gibberish.

3. **Be brief.** After you write a first draft, edit away all unnecessary words.

4. **Maintain your focus.** Keep your goal in mind as you write, and "don't inadvertently open garden gates."

5. **Know your audience.** Provide information in the kind of language your audience will understand.

6. Include data. Make your message stronger with facts and figures to give it focus, dimension, and impact.

— KEY TAKEAWAY —
Writing is an essential life skill that can open doors and attract opportunities in your career. Being able to express yourself makes a big difference in almost any type of work. Even a simple text message must be clearly written and carefully proofed to deliver your point.

Classes can help you brush up on grammar, punctuation, and sentence structure. Many books or online writing tools also can help. And devote more time to reading. Notice the written material you like best, and think about what makes it so effective.

Getting specific, immediate feedback on something you've written can help you improve quickly. One way to get friendly editing is to exchange writing projects with a buddy or a small group of fellow writers.

Most writers will tell you that a key to improving your work is practice, practice, practice. We writers never stop trying to improve. And the more we practice the art and craft of writing, the more fun we have.

Chapter 31

Learn to Move Past Bumps and Stumbles

No matter how hard and smart you work, you will encounter bad days on the job. We all run into bumps and obstacles. Sometimes, though, a career stumble can feel like the end of the world.

When I was a young lawyer, I thought my work had to be perfect. Even a small error might cause me to wake up in the middle of the night, feeling mortified and dreading the next day. The worst was when I unsuccessfully pitched a prospective client. It felt like personal rejection when that person didn't hire me.

Over the years, like every other professional, I had my share of mistakes. I made judgment calls that turned out to be wrong, and sometimes I offended people when I didn't mean to. Then at other times I faced career catastrophes that weren't my fault, like when my employer went out of business.

I gradually got better at moving past setbacks. We get stronger and more resilient when we hit hard times, learn from them, and then keep going. I found ways to put my disappointments and obstacles into perspective. You can too.

THIS YOUNG PROFESSIONAL NEEDED TO FAIL IN ORDER TO GROW

Some people take longer to learn how to brush themselves off and move forward after a career bump. For my client Charlene, the lesson may have been more painful because it came rather late.

Charlene had been a star in college and then sailed through business school. From there she joined the marketing department of a large consumer goods company, where she hoped to quickly snag a management role.

Charlene is clever and determined, so she wasn't surprised when, early in her tenure, she was named team leader for the launch of an exciting new product. She was thrilled by the opportunity and confident the project would succeed. She saw it as her ticket to an early promotion.

But things didn't work out that way. Her team members couldn't seem to agree about how to shape the campaign. Competitors were already using techniques she thought she'd invented. Plus, her young digital marketing experts had trouble relating to a product designed to appeal to older, affluent consumers.

Eventually, the launch team was disbanded, the product was put on a back burner, and Charlene was reassigned to work on routine messaging for one of the company's well-established brands. She was devastated and worried that her marketing career was over. Occasionally, she blamed the situation on her team, but mostly she berated herself for being weak and stupid. Her confidence was gone. Her sense of failure sometimes made her feel sick.

When I met Charlene, I suspected she had breezed through school with what leading psychologist Carol Dweck calls a "fixed mindset." Charlene had always believed her parents when they told her she was destined for business greatness. She saw herself as special, and since childhood, she believed her talent would assure success.

Now, when she couldn't complete this plum assignment, Charlene's shame was overwhelming. She hadn't expected to encounter failure, and she had no idea how to move past it.

YOUR MINDSET CAN SHAPE YOUR
REACTION TO A SETBACK

In her influential book *Mindset: The New Psychology of Success*, Dr. Dweck uses the term *mindset* to describe the attitude you adopt regarding your abilities. Her research suggests your outlook can profoundly impact the way you see yourself and live your life. People with a "fixed" mindset tend to believe that their personal traits are carved into stone.

It's not unusual for people with a *negative* fixed mindset to sabotage their own progress. If you think your abilities are limited, you have a tendency to lower the quality of your work. Even if it's *positive*, a fixed mindset can hinder your ability to bounce back from failure.

Charlene had a confident but inflexible vision of herself. For someone with a fixed self-image like Charlene, failing to achieve an important goal makes her feel like her abilities are broken. It's like she no longer recognizes herself. The resulting pain can be as debilitating as a physical blow.

In contrast, Dr. Dweck says that people with a "growth mindset" never see their skill set or IQ as set. They know humans can cultivate their intelligence and expand their abilities through learning, experience, and help from others. When people with a growth mindset experience a setback, they recognize the disappointing misadventure as a chance to learn, and they get moving again.

Charlene started shifting her attitude and regaining enthusiasm when she recalled how often over the years she'd been able to learn new things. After noticing past recoveries, she realized she could learn from this situation too. She turned her attention to longer-term career goals and created fresh strategies for heading in that direction.

Charlene abandoned the view of her career as a direct path toward a defined outcome and started thinking of it as an interesting and winding process. She realized the team leadership role had been a chance to try out her managerial skills and make them more effective. She also started looking for new opportunities that would allow her to keep growing.

BUILD RESILIENCE BY PRACTICING TECHNIQUES FOR MOVING PAST SLIPUPS

These approaches helped Charlene, and they might work for you:

1. **Talk about it.** Not everything you do on the job will end well. If you never speak of your missteps, their importance may grow in your mind. You can take the agony out of a blunder by bringing it into the light. This doesn't mean prolonged venting. The smart way to talk about a fiasco is to frame it in an objective way. At first Charlene found it difficult to acknowledge she'd made mistakes. She could discuss the project in a positive way after she'd collected data and written a matter-of-fact account of the team's activities.

2. **Know when and how to apologize.** Sometimes projects don't work out, but there's no need to feel apologetic. On the other hand, if you let someone down, made a bad decision, or were insensitive, it might be time to say you're sorry. Here's how:
   - Start by acknowledging precisely what you did.
   - Describe what you will do to make things better and avoid making the same mistake.
   - Keep your comments simple and straightforward.
   - Be prepared to listen to what the injured person has to say.

3. **Ask for suggestions.** Once Charlene developed her report, she took it to her bosses and mentors and asked for

suggestions for doing better next time. The discussions helped her think about her communication style, identify training opportunities, and explore new ways to help her team members collaborate. The humility with which Charlene sought advice improved her relationship with a senior colleague who once regarded her as arrogant.

4. **Look at the entire process.** Seeing the big picture makes it easier to regard your recent disaster as just one phase in a long course of learning and achievement. In *Never Stop Learning,* Professor Bradley Staats says that process-focused learners are more likely to understand that they aren't fixed in their ability to learn. When you study a process, you usually see it was more complicated than you first imagined. As you examine what happened, you start to get beyond the noise and discomfort to better understand how various factors are related and develop new discipline around reaching your objectives.

5. **See how others move past failure.** Many successful leaders have overcome setbacks, and their example can help you navigate your recovery. Charlene read about President Jimmy Carter, who had a humiliating election loss to Ronald Reagan. Carter might have spent years licking his wounds, but instead he found ways to make a difference. He threw himself into addressing homelessness, poverty, and international conflict, and ultimately was awarded the Nobel Peace Prize. If you don't know how to recover from failure, follow the example of President Carter and find ways to add value. Identify aspects of your job where you can become more productive, learn a new skill, or identify a colleague who could use your help. Each time you recall your catastrophe, refocus and take an action step.

6. **Let it go and move on.** People who are good at handling bumps tend to quickly move through these steps:

- Look objectively at the situation and separate the things they can control from the things beyond their reach.
- Ask themselves what they have learned from the situation.
- Cut off any lingering tendency to ruminate about the past or catastrophize about the future.
- Make a plan.

— KEY TAKEAWAY —

Be careful how you talk to yourself about failure. One of the worst parts of a career disaster is when the voice in your head argues that you will never get past it.
That voice is wrong.

Highly successful people tend to take risks, and sometimes things don't work out. Remind yourself that this latest adversity is a key learning experience. Turn your attention to your longer-term goals and values. Then plan a few immediate steps that can move you forward.

Chapter 32

Your Problems May Be the Start of Something Good

The normal successful career is a pattern of ups and downs. *Everyone experiences the downs, like failing at a project, being treated unfairly, losing opportunities because a market crashes, or completely losing interest because you've done the same old thing for too long.*

You're more likely to enjoy life and continue to find satisfaction in your work when you recognize that rough spots are an inevitable part of the process. Often the difficult times help you grow and push you to rise even higher in the next career phase.

FEELING STUCK PUSHED THIS SALES MANAGER FORWARD

Although Adam felt miserable at work, he didn't think he could make a move. Since his college graduation eight years earlier, Adam had worked in sales for a long-established manufacturer. It was the largest private sector employer in the small city where Adam grew up, and he liked the family-friendly, community-focused culture.

Yet Adam worried the company was not preparing for the future. He thought its marketing was stodgy, its product development was unimaginative, and its leaders were resisting change. He also hadn't been shy about expressing his concerns.

Recently, his supervisor had ordered Adam to stay in his lane and stop complaining because people were tired of his meddling and negativity.

Although Adam saw no future for himself at the company, and there were few local jobs, he and his wife were determined to stay in town. They were expecting a baby and hoped to raise her near their supportive families.

When we first spoke, I let Adam vent for a while about how he felt stuck. Then I did what coaches always do: I asked positively worded, open-ended questions intended to help him focus on the future and think in new ways.

Adam acknowledged some good aspects of his job, but he desperately wanted an opportunity to make a bigger contribution. Soon he saw that waiting for somebody to hand him new responsibilities was a waste of time. He could define his own future, which meant making plans and taking steps.

Adam created this plan:

1. **Do his job.** He would remain positive and cheerfully complete all tasks required by his current job description.
2. **Build new skills.** He would build digital marketing and other expertise through online courses.
3. **Offer his expertise.** Within the company he would look for small, specific opportunities for sharing his new skills in a helpful way. At the same time he would explore applying his expertise to a freelance side gig.
4. **Network.** To learn more about the cutting edge in sales and marketing, and also meet potential partners and clients, he would connect with local entrepreneurs and community leaders.

When he launched his plan, Adam didn't know whether he'd stay at the company or launch his own business. He was able to do both.

As soon as Adam found a learning path, he was less frustrated by the narrow scope of his current job. He concentrated on giving his bosses what they wanted, while redirecting his excess energy to mastering new techniques. Creating new skills and seeing a potential path to independence allowed him to look more dispassionately at the company's needs. That helped him spot opportunities for offering help in a humble way, instead of like a know-it-all. His relationships at the company improved quickly.

At the same time, Adam started helping small businesses create social media and digital marketing campaigns. He kept his bosses informed about his side gig, and they became intrigued by what he was doing. Eventually, Adam was promoted to a job with broader scope, with the understanding that he could continue to serve a few small clients on the side.

FEELING BLOCKED CAN SPUR YOU TO MOVE AHEAD

Author Ryan Holiday is skilled at studying the work of ancient philosophers and applying their advice to modern dilemmas. In *The Obstacle Is the Way*, Holiday offers a formula for moving past roadblocks and turning weakness into strength.

Holiday says overcoming obstacles requires three steps:

1. **Perception.** Look at the situation in an objective, unemotional way. Study the big picture and spot opportunities.
2. **Action.** Get moving, learn through trial and error, and keep doing the hard work.
3. **Will.** Resign yourself to grappling with your difficult task without losing hope. Know "the will" is the one thing you control completely. A determination to keep moving allows you to adjust to an unpredictable world by protecting your inner self, aligning with a bigger cause, staying focused, and thriving as you persevere.

— KEY TAKEAWAY —

We all face career difficulties and moments
when we feel like failures. Those difficult times
make us feel uncertain, but they also can push
us to grow and discover new possibilities.

Chapter 33

Grit Gets You through
the Tough Spots

We all hit rough patches, when nothing seems easy or fun, and no relief is in sight. When we stumble or face catastrophes, it's tempting to quit. Yet some people—and not necessarily the most talented people—just keep at it. They don't give up. These people have *grit*.

Grit isn't a fixed quality. You *can* build it, and many people get grittier with time and experience. *There's no easy path because grit is about doing difficult things.*

One of my favorite discussions about how it works is from *Grit & Grace,* an inspiring fitness book written by country music star Tim McGraw.

Apparently, McGraw was in a dark period of life. His dad had died, his relationships weren't going well, and he wasn't fit and healthy. After a wake-up call, he decided to dig himself out of the hole. He committed to a new lifestyle, including a serious exercise program.

McGraw transformed his life and his body, despite the challenges of working out while on tour. He recruited members of his band to join him, and they pushed themselves hard, and not just because they wanted the exercise. McGraw said they completed rigorous workouts in difficult circumstances "because they gave us a training ground for a set of skills that everyday life doesn't always give you a chance to practice: to get uncomfortable, stop thinking, start doing, and build some grit."

According to McGraw, grit "is a combination of focus and perseverance. You call on grit to keep yourself gunning for a personal cause that really matters to you when your ego is telling you to give up or downgrade your ambitions."

Probably the leading academic authority on grit is Angela Duckworth, a University of Pennsylvania psychology professor who knows a lot about character development. She has sold more than a million copies of *Grit: The Power of Passion and Perseverance.*

Duckworth says grit usually involves holding onto a top-level goal—like a "life philosophy"—for a very long time. That might include a conviction that your work matters and a motivation to serve others.

Also important to growing grit is an interest in what you do. She says gritty people don't enjoy everything about their work, but "they're captivated by the endeavor as a whole."

Grit is associated with the capacity to practice. Duckworth says this means you have the daily discipline of trying to do things better than you did yesterday. "To be gritty is to resist complacency. 'Whatever it takes, I want to improve!' is a refrain of all paragons of grit."

HOW CAN *YOU* GET MORE GRIT?

I wish I could offer you an easy formula for becoming grittier. Many of us develop grit through trial and error. Maybe we give up when something we want feels too hard. Then later we look back and see we would have been better off, and happier with ourselves, if we'd kept trying. So the next time we consider quitting, we say to ourselves, "I'll keep going one more day." Then we say the same thing the next day. And as we go on, we build grit.

Sometimes we get grittier because we *have* to, like when there's a serious crisis and other people's jobs, or lives, depend on us. ***You can also develop grit little by little, pushing yourself to keep moving one sugar grain at a time.***

EXERCISE:

Build grit by defining a small routine and sticking with it, no matter what.

This technique for getting grittier is simple. You identify something you want to accomplish in a series of small steps, and you exercise your grit "muscle" by taking every step even when it's uncomfortable or inconvenient.

Here's an example. You want to clean up your workspace a little at a time, so you decide to go through drawers, boxes, and files for fifteen minutes every day for two weeks.

And you do it.

You spend fifteen minutes on the task *every single day*, no matter how busy you are, and even when you don't want to. You build your grit muscle each time you resist the urge to quit.

Chapter 34

Burnt Out? Maybe You're Lonely

If you're struggling to remain positive and energetic at work, your problems may be less about your boss or your job description than you think. Sometimes the reasons people feel negative or exhausted aren't obvious.

One reason you feel low could be that you are one of the millions of Americans suffering from chronic loneliness.

In 2016, Dr. Vivek Murthy, then US Surgeon General, sounded an alarm. He said the nation was "facing an epidemic of loneliness and social isolation," and it was making people sick. He described loneliness as the feeling that comes when you don't have enough social connection, a need that "has become baked into our nervous system."

Since then the situation has gotten worse. A survey in early 2020 by Cigna, the health-care company, revealed that three in five Americans considered themselves to be lonely. Younger people felt more alone than older people, with 72 percent of folks aged eighteen to twenty-two describing themselves as feeling alone.

During COVID-19, with much of the population stuck at home, people became more aware of the dangers of isolation. Employers and policymakers began thinking more seriously about widespread loneliness as both a national health crisis and a workplace challenge.

Relationships with other people are a critical component of your well-being. *The link between social connection and the state of your overall health and happiness is glaringly clear.*

In *Together,* Dr. Murthy says people with rewarding relationships are more likely to recover quickly from illness, build resilience and immunity, and live long lives. Beyond physical health, connected people have more confidence and self-esteem, and they experience lower levels of anxiety and depression than lonely people.

In contrast, the consequences of feeling isolated can be dramatic, including chronic negativity, fearfulness, and disrupted sleep. Loneliness causes stress and inflammation in the body, and it can increase the risk of heart disease, diabetes, joint disease, obesity, and premature death.

On the job, lonely people face issues like diminished cognitive performance, exhaustion, depression, and feelings of disengagement. It's no wonder that lonelier people are less productive than their more connected colleagues, are more likely to take sick days, and may often feel overwhelmed.

YOUR DEVICES MAY CONTRIBUTE TO YOUR LONELINESS

If you sometimes feel isolated, a reliance on social media, texting, and other electronic communication may be part of your problem. In *Back to Human,* workplace expert Dan Schawbel* reported on the chorus of health professionals warning us about the link between technology addiction and loneliness.

Schawbel's concern is significant because after graduating college in 2006 he quickly launched his high-profile career by writing best-selling books about how millennials can build their professional brands using social media.

In our podcast, Schawbel said he created a national reputation as a social media expert but realized later that connecting mainly through media had left him feeling anxious and isolated. Now his mission is to teach his generation that a digital presence is not enough.

In **Back to Human,** *Schawbel warns younger workers that when "we rely on devices to connect with other humans, our relationships become weaker. Replacing human interactions with text messaging makes us lonely and unhappy."* He says that to "be fulfilled at work, committed to our teams, and happy, we need to focus on building deeper relationships with the people around us."

OTHER JOB FACTORS CAN MAKE YOU LONELY

Dependence on technology is not the only way loneliness can be linked to your work situation. Sometimes the structure of your workday is a root cause of your feeling lonesome.

Perhaps you were thrilled by an opportunity to telecommute, but now you feel bored, stale, or forlorn, without regular opportunities to visit with co-workers. The Cigna study reports that remote workers are more likely to feel alone.

Any busy workers, even those in lively offices, may drift into loneliness without noticing that it's happening. Loneliness can sneak up when you're surrounded by other people all day long, from your morning subway ride to your evening grocery stop. You're always in a mob, but maybe you aren't actually connecting with anyone.

In a crowded environment it's tempting to tune out distractions, which might lead to habits like avoiding eye contact, wearing AirPods to escape human voices, and having lunch alone with a book.

In some cases the constraints of your profession leave you feeling cut off from others. In one of our podcasts, Tom Hodson,* a professor, media figure, and former judge, talked about how lonely running a courtroom can feel. He said the public scrutiny can be intense, adding to the pressure of making difficult judicial decisions.

Professional isolation is a necessary part of sitting on the bench, Hodson said. You face serious questions that you aren't permitted to discuss with other people. Yet a sense of being apart from others can carry over to every area of a judge's life. "You can't just turn it on and off," he said. The sense of being separate can touch all your relationships, including those with your family. And the strain can wear you out.

Whatever your profession, even the frantic pace of success may leave you feeling lonely. Perhaps you're living your dream, with a solid job, healthy family, and nice home. Yet you often feel exhausted and unhappy. The pressure to work long hours and also tend to your family can be unrelenting, leaving few opportunities for socializing with friends. If time keeps speeding along, and now you can't remember the last time you spent a few hours chatting with your pals, it may signal a need to rethink your schedule.

FALLING INTO A LONELINESS TRAP CAN DEVASTATE YOUR CAREER

The association between loneliness and professional crises can be complicated and difficult to chart. When my new clients describe their disaffection at work, they seldom use the word *lonely*. Often, as we talk about their unhappiness or lack of productivity, social isolation becomes a recurring theme.

This happened with my client Alice, who wanted help in dealing with burnout and conflict. A year earlier she had accepted a junior leadership post in an organization that seemed friendly. Yet from the start, Alice had been butting heads with her colleagues.

By the time I spoke with her, she regarded her direct reports as disloyal and incompetent, her boss as ineffectual, and many of her peers as hostile. Alice knew she was on shaky ground. Her response was to work long hours, attempting to accomplish more than anyone else. But the more she worked, the more anxious and unpopular she became.

When I asked Alice about the story of her career, she described the difficult years before she took this job. Her sister and mother both passed away. She and her husband moved to a new apartment to be closer to his office; then he left her for another woman. Her mentoring boss retired, and she clashed with his replacement. She responded to all the stress by throwing herself into technical projects she could manage alone, and gradually she lost touch with her small circle of friends.

Alice described feeling sad and isolated at work. However, the more we spoke about her situation, the more clear it became that her sense of isolation had started long before her current job.

In *Loneliness*, William Patrick and John Cacioppo describe how a person can get trapped in a painful loop. Although different people have different needs for connection, we all suffer if our particular requirements for social contact are not met. When a person like Alice is cut off from supportive relationships, she may develop a painful and frightening sense of being abandoned. Then, say Cacioppo and Patrick, she "may begin to see dangers everywhere on the social landscape."

When we view things through a lens of loneliness, other people appear more critical or hostile. The fear can become an expectation, and we stop seeing things clearly. Eventually, we might lose the ability to regulate our own behavior, so we shout or fight, which leaves us more isolated than ever.

Once Alice saw she was trapped in a loneliness cycle, she decided to take action. She explained to her boss that she was struggling with personal problems, and he told her about an employee assistance program that would provide grief counseling.

To strengthen her personal life, Alice joined a nearby church, as well as a neighborhood walking club. At the office she began building new habits to help connect with colleagues. Once she was willing to grapple with her sense of isolation, Alice was able to re-engage at work and start enjoying life again.

LONELINESS CAN THREATEN YOUR HEALTH AND CAREER, BUT YOU *CAN* RECONNECT

Later we explore many ways to build relationships with other people, from nurturing connections you already have, to expanding and diversifying your network. A starting point is to notice your own attitude and behavior patterns. Do you make an effort to interact with other people, or do you find yourself avoiding them? Do you tend to focus your attention on those you are with, or are you often distracted by your phone?

Here are a few ways you might start battling loneliness:

1. **Get more from meetings.** Alice had regarded most meetings as a waste of time. She'd arrive late, work on her own projects during tedious conversations, and leave quickly. Once she saw that meetings are an easy way to get to know people, she changed her routine. Her new style is to arrive early, greet colleagues, and be prepared to join the discussion in a positive way.

2. **Tweak how you treat others.** If you're feeling isolated, examine how you're interacting with the people you see regularly. If you're too busy to smile and say "hello," if you avoid eye contact, or if you hide in your office with the door closed, your attitude is part of the problem. Practice pausing and focusing on other people. Listen to what they say and be alert for opportunities to respond with "thanks" or an offer of help.

3. **Tend existing relationships.** Sometimes you can address that all-alone feeling without meeting new people. Start by developing closer relationships with colleagues and others you know only slightly. When you see folks, smile and ask

how they're doing. Actually *listen* to their responses. And reach out to suggest walks or other activities where you can get to know them better.

— KEY TAKEAWAY —

We all feel lonely some of the time, but we have the power to build connections with other people. When a sense of isolation hits, pause to notice the feeling and perhaps write about it in your journal. Then start to explore small ways to reach out to others.

Chapter 35

We All Need
Positive Relationships

Studying loneliness is not easy because it's so subjective. You can feel lonely in a crowded room or happily connected when you're walking alone down a country road.

Evolutionary scientists like John Cacioppo have a theory about why and how loneliness occurs. *It seems the sense of being lonely—that feeling of wanting social connection—is a cue for action, in the same way feeling thirsty is a cue to get a drink.*

In the early days, humans could find food or escape danger only by banding together. Over many generations, the behaviors that allowed humans to live successfully in groups became inborn survival skills. By now we've evolved with the need and ability to bond with other people. As part of our social nature, we've inherited the feeling of loneliness to warn us when it's time to connect with our kind.

In *Friendship*, Lydia Denworth suggests people *must* be connected with others in order to function. She says, "While there is natural variation in our taste and need for companionship . . . there is a bottom line—a biological need for connection that must be met to achieve basic health and well-being."

Denworth says our "social brain"—which allows us to understand, interact with, and think about other people—is so important that it "takes up a lot of neural real estate."

One thing our brain does well is help us feel, share, and interpret a complex set of emotions—like sympathy and gratitude—that help us make friends. Being able to create friendly relationships is a vital skill. Denworth says, "Being socially adroit—good at creating and maintaining bonds with others—makes us more likely to survive and reproduce successfully."

Although there's much scientists still don't understand about friendship, Denworth says one thing is clear: it's "a matter of life and death. Our longing for friends is carried in our DNA, in how we're wired. Social bonds have the power to shape the trajectories of our lives. And [friendship] is a necessity that is critical to our ability to succeed and thrive."

In other words, to be well and to perform at your best, you need relationships with other people. When you yearn for social contact that's missing from your life, your feeling of loneliness is a signal that it's time for you to reach out. Because other people also value a sense of connection, many will welcome your approach.

LESSONS FROM THE
HARVARD HAPPINESS STUDY

During crises, you may feel what really matters in life are your relationships with other people. If so, you're not alone.

For more than eighty years researchers at the Harvard Study of Adult Development have been tracking the health and well-being of two groups of men. The first cohort included 268 Harvard sophomores. Few of that original group are still alive, but the research has been extended to include their offspring.

The second cohort was added in the 1970s and included 456 Boston inner-city men. Eventually, that group was increased to include their wives.

Over the years researchers closely followed not only the participants' health issues but also other aspects of their lives, from their marriages to their career trajectories. The results from both groups were the same, and the conclusions were overwhelmingly clear. The scientists found that

1. *How happy people are in their relationships has a powerful influence on their health.* Tending to your relationships is a form of self-care, and people who have warm relationships live longer. Social connections are really good for us, and loneliness kills.

2. *Close relationships, more than money or fame, are what keep people happy.* The quality of your close relationships is important, and living in the midst of good, warm relationships protects your well-being.

3. *Good relationships protect not only overall health but more specifically our brains.* Engaging with other people helps us stay cognitively sharp, and feeling isolated is associated with memory decline.

— KEY TAKEAWAY —

The quality of your relationships is critical to your health and happiness. If you want to create a rewarding life and successful career, you should make relationship building a top priority.

Chapter 36

Networking Matters, and It's about Relationships

Our culture places enormous value on the power of individual effort. I agree that each of us has a vast capacity to learn, grow, and create the career and life that we want. *But that does not mean that you should try doing it alone.*

In *Big Potential,* psychologist Shawn Achor says research shows that "achieving our highest potential is not about survival of the fittest; it is **survival of the best fit** . . . [S]uccess is not just about how creative or smart or driven you are, but how well you are able to connect with, contribute to, and benefit from the ecosystem around you."

Achor says Big Data now allows researchers to see connections that once were hidden. Analysis shows that your greatest successes don't exist in isolation. He says, "As the research begins to emerge, we seem to be learning that almost every attribute of your potential—from intelligence to creativity to leadership to personality and engagement—is interconnected with others."

The evidence is overwhelming. *A key to thriving at work, and in your whole life, is to regularly connect with other people.*

NETWORKING IS ESSENTIAL FOR YOUR CAREER

When I speak with new clients, I try to assess the strength of their networks. I know their professional connections have an immense impact on their work life and potential for success. Often we talk at length about strategies for building those relationships.

Sometimes clients resist my push, saying they're sick of people telling them to network. Do you feel like that?

Well, get over it. *Networking is critical to your happiness and career success.*

Before discussing why it matters to professional success, let's talk about the meaning of *networking*. To begin, let's explore why the term might creep you out.

One reason you might feel unease is that the word *networking* seems to imply using people for your own gain. To some, it sounds like you're about to be selfish or manipulative. But that's not how networking works.

Definitions of *networking* vary, but a common one is something like: "meeting people and sharing information and services for mutual benefit, often in the context of your career." That's close, and the word *mutual* hints at the reciprocal nature of the activity.

The definition is more complete when we add an important word: *relationships.*

The essence of networking is *connecting* with other humans. So let's define it as "building a diverse collection of *relationships* for the purpose of sharing information, services, and support."

Let's be clear: the foundation of networking is each person's need to be connected with other people. We are inherently social, and networking is about developing beneficial social relationships of all sorts, from casual acquaintances to close and enduring friendships. The wider and more varied your collection of relationships, the more they provide support for your professional interests and help you be happier at work.

WHY NETWORKING MATTERS SO MUCH

Now that we've defined networking, let's look at reasons it is so important for your professional life:

1. **Connected people are more fit for work.** Research says that in addition to enjoying better health, connected people have

more confidence and self-esteem, and they experience lower levels of anxiety and depression. Also, they are less likely to suffer from chronic negativity, fearfulness, disrupted sleep, or disengagement at work.

2. **Networking makes you stand out.** If you know many people, others tend to notice. When you are widely recognized, observers see you as capable and influential. Being connected with successful people can enhance your status.

3. **Networking brings opportunities.** Any good networker knows that when you are out and about, meeting other people, you frequently spot opportunities. Maybe you hear about somebody needing a speaker and you snag an invitation that will help raise your profile. Or you're alerted to an opening that would be great for a friend who needs a job. If you become a connector, bringing other people together, you can develop a tremendous reserve of goodwill that will always be there when you need it.

4. **Most jobs are found through relationships.** Surveys say networking is the dominant method used by successful job seekers. More than 70 percent of the time, winning searches involve a referral or other human intervention, and not simply the workings of an automated system. One reason is that most of the job market is hidden, with many spots filled internally or through referrals, without ever being posted. Even when a job is advertised, connected people have an advantage and may get early notice of an opening.

5. **Connected people get powerful references.** Whether you're seeking a job or pitching a client, someone writing a glowing message about your work is helpful. A recommendation carries more weight if it comes from a person who is known and trusted by your target organization. The more people you know, the more likely you can identify a shared contact who is willing to speak up for you.

6. **Wide networks create broader perspectives.** Having extensive professional contacts puts you in the flow of information about things like market shifts, regulatory developments, and technical innovations. If you participate in multiple communities, you may spot developing trends and speak with deeper insight about the future of your field. Even brief interactions with other experts can bring you inspiration and breakthroughs.

7. **Networking can be satisfying and fun.** When marketing consultant Bob Shaff* walks through a room of strangers, you can see he's a master networker. Bob interacts with person after person, asking gentle questions and helping each one relax and engage. He obviously knows how to build relationships. But Bob didn't start out that way. As a young engineer at IBM, Bob was painfully shy and felt isolated. Then IBM taught him sales skills, and he learned connecting with other people is deeply rewarding. Today, he says, meeting other people is a source of endless joy.

— KEY TAKEAWAY —

There's no way around it: networking is crucial
to your work life. The more widely connected
you are, the more you will grow as a professional,
attract career opportunities, and flourish.

Chapter 37

Your Network Provides
Circles of Support

When I was a young lawyer, few women worked in Washington law firms like the one that hired me. Aware that some firm leaders were skeptical about women's ability to carry the load, I was determined to outwork my male colleagues. For the first few months I stuck to my desk, declining evening invitations and concentrating on billing more hours than my peers.

That was a mistake.

Eventually, I felt secure enough to look around and see how things worked. I realized lawyers had to be competent to survive in that environment, but the most successful ones also were good at socializing. Finally, I understood that networking is how lawyers spot trends and find new clients, jobs, and other opportunities.

Once I saw how it all worked, I started cautiously making an effort to meet more people. *Yet I didn't feel enthusiastic about creating a robust network until I began thinking of it as a web of interconnected, authentic, and supportive human relationships.*

Now I love my network. It feels like a living, comforting presence, always there when I am ready to tackle a challenge. My network helps me shift careers, grow businesses, learn new skills, help others, and meet wonderful friends.

Now, as a coach, I closely observe my clients' networking activities and am often reminded of how an extensive collection of contacts translates into career success. *I see some professionals get better at expanding and nurturing their relationships once they develop a mental image of how their network is organized.*

EMPOWER YOUR SOCIALIZING BY ENVISIONING YOUR NETWORK CIRCLES

If you're ready to strengthen your network, pause to imagine how it will look as it grows. *A good way to visualize your network is as a series of concentric circles, spreading out around you like the web of a spider.* You might think of your network as five circles:

1. **The innermost ring includes your closest friends and family.** Introverts particularly enjoy their time here, but even with besties you can't take things for granted. So nurturing this central group requires you to make an effort to stay in touch.

2. **Beyond your core group are newer friends and old friends you seldom see.** These might include co-workers, neighbors, and people you see at routine social events. Asking questions and showing interest are good ways to cultivate this crowd. If you don't strive to grow the relationships, though, it's all too easy for these people to drift away.

3. **The third group includes dozens, hundreds, or even more people from over the years.** Among them are kids from school, co-workers from a while back, fitness classmates, and neighbors who wave on the street. Also here are folks you've never actually seen, like colleagues located across the country or the new spouses of old friends. This circle is a rich source of professional contacts with whom you're seldom in touch—but could be. *When you're starting a job search or looking for other support, this big circle of casual contacts is particularly important.* Your closest friends tend to hear the same news you hear. But your third circle is tight enough to give you real connection yet broad enough to bring new opportunities.

4. **Your network expands when you include people in shared communities.** Maybe you've never met, but you belong to the same organizations, went to the same college, or share some history. You all have something in common because the essence of a community is that it's a *group with members*, rather than a random collection of unconnected people. *Savvy networkers know people often respond warmly to fellow community members, even when they haven't met.* An easy starting point is reaching out to alumni from your college, or "employer alumni" who once worked in the same places you did.

5. **Your social media contacts may include thousands of people who share your interests.** In your fifth circle, you're playing long shots. But don't discount the possibilities here. I've found clients and friends through sites like LinkedIn. I've also "met" readers around the world through Twitter (find me @beverlyejones).

One reason to create a mental picture of your network is that the image reminds you to establish a steady pace as you connect with people both near and far. Powerful networking is pursued gradually and methodically. You think about the many types of potential connections, and you establish a regular routine of reaching out, one sugar grain at a time.

If you're ready to broaden your network, get gritty and promise yourself that every day for one month you'll spend at least a few minutes on outreach activities. When you discipline yourself to maintain a steady pace, you'll become increasingly creative and the process will get easier as you go along.

EXERCISE:

Define the circles of your network. Visualizing various sorts of relationships will suggest new ways to connect and remind you to keep at it. You can borrow my five-ring model or define the categories that work best for you.

To illustrate the full scope of your network, create a map. Draw a series of concentric circles, with your name placed in the middle, like a bull's-eye. Label the rings, moving from your closest loved ones out toward your most distant connections. Once the image is in place, test out the model by contacting one person in each of the rings.

Chapter 38

Networking Isn't about Being Selfish

The essence of networking is getting to know new people, turning acquaintances into friends, and nurturing friendships you already have.

Sometimes networking means attending professional events or working with websites. *But often networking involves engaging with people throughout the normal course of your life, whether you're at the gym or in a meeting.* In any gathering there are ways to connect, and you never know when your efforts will lead to friendships or opportunities.

Perhaps you dread the thought of meeting and greeting, chatting and mingling? Most of us sometimes feel awkward or shy in social situations. It gets easier as you build skills and practice moving a bit out of your comfort zone. A good starting point is to focus your attention on the people around you.

APPROACH NETWORKING
WITH A GENEROUS SPIRIT

Effective networking requires being alert to the needs of other people. *A tried-and-true way to build and care for relationships is to find ways to be helpful.* Here are some of my favorite approaches:

1. **Start where you are.** Expanding your connections means not only meeting new folks but also firming up existing relationships. You can jump-start your networking by reaching out to people in the places where you already hang out.

My client Amara decided to chat more often with her yoga classmates. Her first effort led to a coffee date, and now she has a new friend.

2. **Show up.** Whether it's a party or a meeting, staging an event can be challenging. It's disheartening when few people come. Often you can do something kind, and build a relationship at the same time, by saying "yes" to invitations. Once you have agreed to attend, never ghost a host. It's rude, and hosts seldom forget no-shows.

3. **Say "thank you."** A powerful way to connect with others is to thank them for something. When you sincerely express appreciation, you make someone else feel good, and you feel better, too. If you're routinely polite, kind, and appreciative, people will remember and want to be near you.

4. **Find a helpful role.** When you decide to be more strategic about networking, you may join professional groups, attend local events, or head to conferences. Being in a crowd of strangers can be intimidating and exhausting. But you can ease your stress at gatherings by volunteering to help. If you join the planning committee, you'll know a few people by the time of the event.

5. **Make matches.** A "connector" is a person who matches needs and resources and makes helpful introductions. Perhaps you meet someone moving to a city where your friend needs volunteers for a nonprofit. By making an email intro, you can help two people at once. People remember and turn to connectors, so their networks keep expanding.

6. **Cheer them on.** If an acquaintance does something well, show you noticed and offer congratulations. Don't be afraid to express respect and affection, and be willing to share their excitement.

7. **Notice rough patches.** If you see somebody has hit hard times, don't wait for them to call you. Assume they'd help

you, so reach out. If you frequently support other people, you'll find it easier to seek assistance when you're the one struggling.

8. **Volunteer.** One of the best ways to build connections is by volunteering. A massive 2019 study in Britain concluded that people who volunteer for nonprofit activities find new friends and have fun.

   - Almost 90 percent of volunteers said they met new people.
   - About 76 percent of people thirty-four and younger said volunteering helped them feel less isolated.
   - More than three-fourths reported improved mental health and well-being.
   - Most volunteers cited benefits that matched their initial reasons for volunteering, like meeting people. They also reported additional benefits, like enjoying the experience.

— KEY TAKEAWAY —

Connecting with other people is something you can learn. The more you practice reaching out in a kind way, the easier networking becomes. In each situation, start by setting your attitude, reminding yourself that these people may be as shy as you, and wishing them well.

Chapter 39

LinkedIn Networking
Tips from an Expert

Creating relationships face-to-face is an irreplaceable survival skill.

Smart career networkers also understand how to use digital technologies to meet new people, deepen relationships, and stay in touch. For professionals, the premier tool is LinkedIn, a career-focused social networking site owned by Microsoft.

You can get started on LinkedIn, free, in just a couple of hours. But mastering all the possibilities is complicated. The site offers layers of features that allow users to share experiences and resumes, find jobs, and make friends. So it's good to have help.

My favorite LinkedIn expert is widely quoted Susan P. Joyce*. She has been teaching, writing, and speaking about how to run online job searches ever since she was laid off in 1994. For more than twenty years Susan has been editor of *Job-Hunt.org*, a robust employment portal (where I write about networking).

Susan combines a deep empathy for career builders with a sophisticated understanding of how to make good use of LinkedIn's extraordinary power. I asked her to share her top ten LinkedIn networking tips.

ESSENTIAL ADVICE FROM SUSAN JOYCE

First, Susan says, avoid making the mistake of assuming LinkedIn is irrelevant if you're happily employed. Most people today check LinkedIn quickly before meeting you for the first time, or they'll go to the site after you've met. If you have a solid presence on LinkedIn, your next employer might find you, even if you aren't looking for a new job.

Susan offered one cautionary note: *If you are employed, check to see if your employer has a social media policy governing employees, which may impact your use of sites like LinkedIn.*

Here are more tips from Susan:

1. **Be identifiable.** Your name (consistently use the same version), photograph, job title/profession, and location are essential parts of your profile, and they help prove that you and your profile are not fake. Also, they make it easy for people to find you and contact you on LinkedIn.

2. **Maximize visibility.** Be sure that your LinkedIn privacy settings allow your full name and your profile to be visible both inside and outside of LinkedIn. If your whole name isn't visible, your profile will be hard to find unless someone is already connected to you. The privacy settings also allow you to limit your profile's visibility to people who start a search elsewhere, such as Google. If you block your profile from being visible outside LinkedIn, a Google search for your name will not find your profile, making you harder to locate.

3. **Be reachable.** A fabulous LinkedIn profile is not especially useful if there is no way for people *outside* of LinkedIn to contact you. Not everyone can send messages via the site's InMail. And if you are seldom active on LinkedIn, you may not see InMail that is sent to you. Include your information not only in your LinkedIn "Contact info" section, but also in your "About" section, since the contact information is usually visible only to people connected to you in some way.

4. **Protect your privacy.** Susan's recommendation is to use Gmail and Google Voice accounts for your contact information. Both can be forwarded to your primary accounts, while protecting your real contact information from public

view. LinkedIn also asks for your address. *Do not provide your home address, even if you are unemployed.* Your work address or, better, simply a city and state, or a generic name like "greater Boston area" is sufficient. In addition, *LinkedIn asks for your birthday. Skip this!* This information helps identity thieves.

5. **Don't have a skimpy profile—make your current (and former) jobs and employers clear.** *Complete* your profile. Share your professional background to help people see what you might have in common with them and how you might fit into their professional network. Share up to fifteen or twenty years of your work history in the "Experience" section, describing each job and employer with an emphasis on aspects relevant today.

6. **Make your schools and qualifications clear.** Even if you didn't graduate, share the schools you attended, along with your major and/or degrees, without necessarily including the years of attendance. Also include any relevant professional certifications and licenses.

7. **Make your professional qualifications and expertise clear.** In the "Featured" section at the top of your profile, add links to content you have written or created. Write articles on LinkedIn, and link to them in this section. Also share job-related content posted on other sites, like articles published on other websites, posts in your own blog, or content published on a site like SlideShare. Before publishing or linking to any of your content, be sure to remove anything an employer might consider confidential.

8. **Expand your LinkedIn network.** Focus on growing your network—reach out to people with whom you share schools or employers, people who work for your target employers, people who have the same or similar professions, people who share posts you like, recruiters, and more. Do NOT limit

your LinkedIn network only to people you have met in person! Grow your network on LinkedIn by *carefully* accepting connection invitations from people you don't (yet) know.

9. **Don't confuse LinkedIn with Facebook or a dating site.** *Some people do not understand that LinkedIn is the professional network*, and they tell you how stupid you are or, conversely, how attractive you are. The best strategy is to ignore and/or block those members, and not make the same mistakes yourself. *Remember, everything you do or write on LinkedIn is usually visible to the world*, so focus on presenting your best self—positive and professional.

10. **Be active.** Spend at least 10 or 15 minutes a day on LinkedIn (more if you are in a job search), reading and reacting to your "Notifications." Demonstrate your knowledge and expertise. "Follow" people who post or publish interesting information. Share good information in comments or thank others for sharing good information.

— KEY TAKEAWAY —

LinkedIn is a major resource for any professional interested in connecting with other professionals. People will check you out once they have met you or heard of you. If you're not on the site, people may track you down elsewhere online, and you'll have no control over what they find.

For more tips, follow Susan on LinkedIn: *www.linkedin.com/in/susanjoyce/*.

While you're there, you can follow me: *www.linkedin.com/in/beverly-jones-coach-author/*.

Chapter 40

Broad, Diverse Networks Take You Further

Becoming a strong networker requires more than adding names to your address book. *You'll get more from your circles of connection if they encompass a wide variety of people.*

In *Big Potential*, Shawn Achor says, "From evolutionary theory, we know that the key to survival is biodiversity. . . . By the same token, the more diverse your social support network, the more resilient you will be when life throws you a curveball."

Scientists who study patterns of human connection say that an "open," varied network is a key predictor of career success.

It's not unusual for people to feel more comfortable in networks that are "closed," meaning they often hang out with the same crowd. If most people you know share an occupation, religion, or political party, chances are your network is closed. With a limited network, you tend to encounter people with similar backgrounds, educations, and interests.

In the short term, life might feel easy in your closed network, where people seldom challenge your assumptions. But you'll miss countless chances to expand your knowledge, notice emerging trends, escape the dangers of groupthink, and bump into surprising opportunities.

An open network can help you understand evolving trends, connect with more professional communities, and build a clearer view of the big picture. As you expand your web of connection, you may become more innovative and creative.

One practical benefit is that people with diverse networks are more likely to find good jobs. Having a variety of acquaintances makes it easier for you to hear about openings, obtain references, and prepare for interviews. Research says people with more network variety land the jobs with higher rank and income.

HOW TO BROADEN YOUR NETWORK

Maybe you've been working hard to add connections to your LinkedIn account and now I tell you that's good, but it's not quite enough to maximize your learning and opportunities.

Hear me out!

All the work you've done so far has helped you meet people and build your social skills. *Now it's time to use those networking skills in a wider range of situations.*

I know stepping beyond your comfort zone can be daunting. Most of us sometimes feel intimidated by unfamiliar groups. *Homophily* is the term used to describe the common tendency for humans to link up with each other in ways that confirm our core beliefs and worldviews. It's a sociologist's way of saying that "birds of a feather flock together," and people often feel safer in familiar communities.

But you can widen your circles without doing anything too scary. *As with any project, you can start opening your network with a series of tiny steps. Begin by articulating your intention to engage with a more diverse collection of people.*

Remind yourself of that intent any time you're out and about. When you're at a gathering, look around for someone who seems different from your normal crowd, and introduce yourself to that person. To make it more likely you'll encounter a wider mix of people, vary your routines and attend events outside your norm. Try taking a class. Or join a group based on an interest not related to your job, like a sport, your neighborhood, or a charity.

SUPPORT DIVERSITY IN YOUR WORKPLACE

An effective way to broaden your circles is to spend time with people who have varied networks. That includes working in a diverse environment.

Overwhelming evidence suggests diversity and equal opportunity in the workplace can be assets for both employers and their employees. The coming together of people with varied backgrounds, ethnicities, and skills drives innovation and organizational resilience. People with different experience and viewpoints tend to see the same problem in different ways, increasing the odds of successful solutions.

This is not to say that managing diversity is always easy. Sometimes working in a multicultural environment is challenging because people with dissimilar backgrounds don't always get along. There have been some disappointing results from the first generation of institutional programs intended to promote diversity and inclusion (known as "D&I").

Years ago, during the first major push for equal career opportunity, many of us assumed that if diverse categories of people are hired, eventually they'll all work well together. My longtime friend Rob Jones*, an executive coach and D&I expert, says it's not been that simple.

Today's organizations often include people from a broad variety of cultural backgrounds, but not everyone's voice carries the same weight. Jones says it's time to move past old-fashioned programs in which people are ordered to ignore human differences, and concentrate on creating cultures where everyone is welcome, all voices are invited, and collaboration is rewarded.

A simple way to support inclusion is to regularly reach out to colleagues, check in, and listen to what they say.

A sincere belief in inclusion and goodwill is not always enough. In a podcast conversation, Dayna Bowen Matthew*, dean of George Washington University Law School and author of *Just Medicine*, said **often inequities are built into the norms and systems of our institutions, even where there is a genuine intent to treat people equally.** Sometimes the problem stems from policies, like those about appearance, holiday schedules, or business-related social events. At other times cultural assumptions shape how people interact.

— KEY TAKEAWAY —

The more diverse your network, the stronger and more resilient it will be. Having too many similar folks in your circles means you miss out on all kinds of opportunities. Cultivate a wider range of contacts by varying your routines and connecting with new people wherever you go.

Chapter 41

Quit Taking Things So Personally

One reason we dread networking is we worry about being rejected. Whether we're approaching someone we know, or we're gathering the nerve to speak to a stranger, we suddenly think, "Oh! I don't want to bother them."

If an encounter becomes awkward, we might feel mortified, asking ourselves, "Why am I such an idiot?"

Many of us have this experience because humans are hardwired to overreact to anything that feels threatening or risky. As social beings, we yearn for approval from the people around us and cringe at the thought of not belonging.

Although we are born with these common fears, we also have the power to be less worried about rejection.

NETWORKERS CAN GET COMFORTABLE WITH A LITTLE REJECTION

Unless you suffer from serious social anxiety, acquiring the skill of rolling with the social punches is easier than it sounds. I learned this from years in crowded rooms with public officials, sometimes as the least important person in the room.

In reality, our inbred fear of social rejection is often worse than the actual experience of being casually rejected. Sure— worrying about being intrusive or unwelcome feels excruciating. But I promise that actually being snubbed doesn't need to be too painful.

You seldom lose much when other people don't want to talk with you. They don't know you, maybe they are anxious or busy, and typically a rude encounter is more about them than about you.

People who become adept at working a room know it's a numbers game. You don't need to be accepted by everyone or even most people. As with sales, the process of building connections means trying more than once.

When you attend enough events, you learn to move quickly from encounters that don't produce a good fit. The trick is to refocus on the next stranger, and chances are they feel just as shy as you do.

BOUNCE BACK FROM RUDENESS OR CRITICISM

Our desire for respect and acceptance translates into a tendency to feel hurt when others are rude, insulting, or dismissive.

At networking events rejection doesn't have to hurt so much because it's easier to dismiss the behavior of strangers. *In the workplace, where we try so hard to succeed, even legitimate criticism of our performance sometimes feels too personal, like a kick in the gut.*

Because human brains tend to overfocus on negative events, critical comments may have the power to bring you down, attack your confidence, or reduce your motivation. It's not unusual to overrespond to criticism, even when most other feedback about your work is positive.

Some people have a particularly hard time moving past any kind of emotional wound. They think repeatedly about mean remarks and dwell endlessly on moments of unfairness or disrespect.

Ruminating over unkind or negative conversations can throw you into a downward spiral. Carrying around hurt feelings can make you overly sensitive to even casual remarks. Once you get into a defensive mode, it's difficult to do your best work. Your colleagues, wanting to avoid the drama, may be reluctant to offer helpful suggestions.

Enjoying work is much easier if you can quickly release any pain associated with criticism or rudeness. A wise response is to listen for useful suggestions buried within the negativity, refocus on your future work, and let go of your reaction to anything that feels too personal. The letting-go part takes effort.

For clients struggling to deal with negativity, I sometimes recommend *The Four Agreements*, by don Miguel Ruiz.

Based on ancient Toltec teachings, Ruiz's book describes four "agreements"—deals you make with yourself about what to feel and how to behave in certain situations. He says if you adopt these four practices, you can avoid a lot of suffering.

Ruiz's Second Agreement is: "Don't take anything personally. Nothing others do is because of you. What others say and do is a projection of their own reality, their own dream."

Ruiz explains, "When you take things personally, then you feel offended, and your reaction is to defend your beliefs and create conflicts. You make something big out of something so little, because you have the need to be right and make everybody else wrong."

I agree with Ruiz that not taking things so personally can be life changing. *Shifting your perspective and recognizing that small things don't have to matter can help you avoid pain and transform how you engage with other people.*

Dealing with disapproval and hostility is a learnable skill. These techniques can help you cope with unkindness or negativity:

1. **Find a few words.** Come up with a phrase—like "it's more them than me"—and repeat it to yourself when feeling bruised by someone's comment. The more often you repeat

this mantra, the faster it will come to mind when you're in a difficult conversation.

2. **Write about it.** You'll move past the hurt more quickly if you journal about the situation. Describing the pain helps you let it go. Writing dispassionately about ugly comments allows you to care less about the malicious language and perhaps spot some grains of truth. Even cruel comments may contain information to help you up your game.

3. **Be mindful.** Meditation and other mindfulness techniques can help reduce your stress after a difficult encounter. For example, if you try meditative music or guided imagery, your anger and gloom may slip away as your body relaxes.

4. **Succeed elsewhere.** A stinging comment can upset you by undercutting your confidence. It can help to change gears and do something you're good at. Another response is to exercise intensely; trying hard at the gym can make you feel successful and confident.

— KEY TAKEAWAY —

Much of what people say about others is a reflection of their own mood, goals, and struggles. If you keep reminding yourself to not take things so personally, you can learn to feel calmer. Knowing how to bounce back from rudeness and negativity means other people have less power to hurt you.

Chapter 42

Embrace the Joys and Benefits of Mentoring

Over the years, mentoring relationships have brought me joy and learning. Besides my personal experience, as a coach and executive I've been able to observe many mentors in action.

The typical setup starts with an experienced person who is asked to guide a junior, less-knowledgeable colleague. Many organizations have experimented with formal programs, where mentors are matched with lower-ranking mentees to support their professional development.

Some structured programs have mixed results, since the relationships don't always seem to click. Usually, however, there are advantages for both partners, including these:

1. **Knowledge transfer.** Mentoring is a fast way to help employees get started in new organizations or positions. The mentees benefit from having an accessible source of expert guidance. Because teachers tend to learn along with their students, mentors also may deepen their expertise and broaden their perspective.

2. **Career development.** One-on-one partnerships can be an excellent way to help junior colleagues learn about an organization's culture, goals, and expectations. It's helpful when a person—*other than your boss*—talks clearly and directly about the keys to your success. The mentor may also serve as a role model, with the protégée learning by observation as well as through conversation.

3. **Diversity and inclusion.** Organizations can support innovation by creating opportunities for senior employees to gather new ideas from members of underrepresented groups. Mentors can help mentees develop confidence and pursue strategies for growth and advancement. Both partners can explore leadership and other challenges during relaxed conversations about everything from networking to embedded bias.

MY EXPERIENCE WITH MENTORING HAS BEEN FUN AND REWARDING

Mentoring has been a major theme in my career, beginning back when large numbers of women were just starting to enter professional fields like law. We needed help to make our way in occupations where not everyone wanted us to be successful. Once we got inside the doors, most of us pushed hard to support the broad waves of women who were right behind us.

When the match feels right, I've always loved serving as an informal mentor. It's fun brainstorming about the logistics of career success. I learn from looking at work situations from another's perspective. Some mentoring relationships gradually become deep friendships, full of laughter as well as serious talk.

An important early insight was that mentoring is about building real, human relationships, and most relationships work best when they are reciprocal. In other words, the old-fashioned model of a wise senior offering wisdom to an avid junior colleague works only for a little while. *What makes a partnership powerful and long-lasting is that each partner both teaches and learns.*

One of my longtime mentoring relationships is with Gayle Williams-Byers, the judge described previously. She interned for me in Washington during college, after graduation she joined my team for a year, and then my employer's scholarship program assisted her in law school.

Gayle showed me how powerful mentoring can be, because even after she left my professional orbit, she refused to let go. She said both of us had invested substantial time and energy in this relationship, and in her view we were committed for life.

These days, Gayle and her husband, Greg, regularly make the long drive from Cleveland to visit our Virginia farmhouse. We speak openly about most things, without judgment or obligations. We still have a teach-and-learn relationship, but these days she is more often the teacher.

Not every mentoring partnership needs to be intense. Sometimes a few quick chats are all it takes to create a friendly connection that both people enjoy, find rewarding, and may call on in the future.

These suggestions can help you develop mentoring relationships:

1. **Start slow.** Whether you're seeking assistance or want to be helpful, don't push too hard in the beginning. If you don't know each other well, blunt offers or requests for mentoring can be off-putting. When you're recruiting assistance, start with a small, explicit request. If you spot a potential mentee, initiate your outreach with a low-key invitation like, "Do you want to grab a coffee?"

2. **Embrace honesty.** Your mentor's most important contribution can be providing unbiased, constructive feedback, even when it's not easy for you to hear. If you're working on a project where your mentor has expertise, seek specific suggestions. Resist any urge to respond defensively, and express appreciation for tough advice.

3. **Touch base.** If you connect only when the mentee is in trouble, the relationship may fade away. In the best relationships the partners stay in touch, checking on each other

from time to time, and talking about their successes as well
as failures.

4. **Help and give back.** In a lasting relationship, mentor and
mentee look out for one another. As years go by, they share
useful information and find ways to connect each other
with interesting people. They offer support in both good
times and bad.

5. **Notice where the joy is.** Most people like to be helpful.
and they also need to feel respected and appreciated. What
makes mentoring relationships special is the regular exchange of kindness and gratitude, nurturing and respect.

— KEY TAKEAWAY —

**Mentoring relationships can enrich your life
and enhance career success. The best mentoring
partnerships are reciprocal, with both people learning
and sharing information. In lasting relationships,
both partners enjoy the time spent together and
remain interested in each other's activities.**

Chapter 43

Self-Confidence Starts with Action

A lack of confidence can hold you back and make you miserable at work. When you're not sure of yourself, you might hesitate to connect with other people. You're less likely to go after challenging projects. When leaders or clients sense your lack of assurance, they may hesitate to offer challenging assignments, even if you're the most qualified person.

CONFIDENCE IS HARD TO DESCRIBE, BUT YOU KNOW WHEN YOU NEED IT

What is self-confidence? When you feel confident, you believe in yourself. You recognize that you have the ability to wrestle with problems and find a way to succeed.

Feeling confident doesn't mean you're arrogant. You don't have an exaggerated sense of your own importance, or feel superior and entitled.

In *How to Have a Good Day*, management consultant Caroline Webb says, "Real confidence doesn't have to be about talking loudly. It's more about being the person we are when we're at our best, rather than trying to copy what we think self-assurance looks like in someone else."

Self-confident people don't waste time comparing themselves with the competition. They understand their own strengths and values, and when a challenge comes along, they jump in and stick with it. Of course, that doesn't mean confident people are never afraid; it's more a matter of not letting fear hold you back.

FOUR TIMES I FOUND SELF-CONFIDENCE

Perhaps like you, I've had periods when I lacked confidence. At times I couldn't shake the sense of not being good enough. *To illustrate a few ways you can find self-confidence, I describe four of those other times, when I managed to dig deep and keep going:*

1. **Focusing on a mission makes you strong.** I've mentioned that period in my twenties when I led university women's programs. I didn't have the expertise or experience for a leadership role, but that didn't bother me because I wasn't focused on my personal career. At that time, I was driven by a vision of equal opportunity for all, and I paid little attention to what other people thought of me.

2. **Self-talk influences your confidence level.** After the OU years, I headed to law school in Washington. When I compared myself to my accomplished and socially secure fellow students, my confidence plummeted. A negative voice in my head made me feel like a loser. However, everything changed when I replaced that voice with more positive self-talk. Learning to maintain an optimistic attitude was life changing and gave me the confidence to push forward even when I was scared.

3. **Expertise leads to confidence.** As a young lawyer I put in long hours learning and practicing my craft. Along the way I made mistakes but found ways to sort things out and keep going. Gradually, my efforts brought me skill and experience, and with them the confidence that comes from knowledge.

4. **Say "yes" and confidence may follow.** When I shifted careers from law to coaching, I missed feeling like an expert. I was acutely aware of being a novice again, this time in a field still being invented. When I marketed myself as a coach, people asked questions like, "Could you give us this

training?" or "Can you help that person?" My first reaction was often to think, "No! I don't know how." Then I made a promise to myself: whenever someone proposed a project, I would respond, "Yes! I will send a proposal." By saying "yes," I gained some time to manage my fear. And I gradually built confidence as I repeatedly invented proposals.

DOING SOMETHING IS BETTER THAN DOING NOTHING

In *The Confidence Code,* authors Katty Kay and Claire Shipman examine the nagging self-doubt that burdens many women at all levels of achievement. Not surprisingly, their research confirms that without confidence you won't achieve your highest level of success. The impact is bigger than your career because confidence "is an essential element of internal well-being and happiness for a fulfilled life."

There seems to be a spiral. When it's flowing downward, you lack confidence, and without confidence, you can't be truly happy in your work. If you're unhappy, you're less likely to succeed, which drives your confidence down even further.

So how do you *get* confidence?

According to Kay and Shipman, qualities like optimism are important. The real magic happens, though, when you step beyond your comfort zone. They say all their research leads to this conclusion: *"Nothing builds confidence like taking action, especially when the action involves risk and failure. Risk keeps you on life's edge. It keeps you growing, improving and gaining confidence."*

I agree that *doing* something is the way to cultivate confidence. At times that might mean something huge, like accepting a challenging new job even when you feel totally unprepared.

Often you don't need to make a big bold move to get going. The amount of risk it takes to trigger an upward spiral can be tiny. *Your first action step can be as simple as writing in your journal. The key is to keep going.* The little burst of confidence that comes each time you make a small effort contributes to the amazing power of gradual change. Each sugar grain of action adds to your store of confidence and helps you move along.

So here's your upward spiral: your action brings a small success, which brings confidence, which leads to the next positive action, which brings more confidence.

The actions you take can change how you think about yourself. And what you do can become who you are.

As you build confidence in one area of your life, the change can flow over to others. Often with clients I've seen how becoming more physically fit or doing well in charitable activities results in an improved attitude at work. If you're pleased with your performance in leisure activities, your self-assurance helps set you up for success on the job.

EXERCISE:

As a step toward greater confidence, journal about your challenges, goals, and special strengths. A good starting point is to write about three of your good points. A friend who teaches positive psychology uses writing exercises to help her students become more confident by noticing their strengths. It can be challenging at first.

She says, "I have been making my students write an essay where they must describe three positive attributes about themselves, whether it is about their creativity, kindness, good listening skills, or athletic abilities. I thought it would be easy, but *many* students start their paper saying they are embarrassed to be writing such things. Or they wish I had asked about three areas where they need to improve. Or they have never thought about it."

Chapter 44

Get Past Boredom

Although most of us have our own idea about what feeling bored means, the concept of "boredom" is hard to pin down. The experience varies from person to person, and sometimes it gets tangled up with other conditions, like depression or exhaustion.

There are different kinds of boredom. Maybe you're in a meeting with colleagues having the same old argument and you start to feel trapped, restless, and eager to do anything but listen to this one more time.

Sometimes you're not experiencing boredom so much as missing a habitual stimulus. Perhaps you usually check your phone throughout the day. Each time you spot a message, your body responds with a little hit of adrenalin, and eventually your phone habit can operate like an addiction. When you're in a setting where devices aren't permitted, missing that adrenalin makes you feel antsy and bored, even if the topic under discussion matters to your work.

On the job, boredom seems to be the opposite of what psychologist Mihaly Csikszentmihalyi labeled "flow." When we are in a flow state, he wrote, we are totally involved, and "action follows upon action according to an internal logic that seems to need no conscious intervention by the actor."

You are most likely to feel deeply engaged in work, and not bored, when your tasks require effort, skill, commitment, and learning. Cures for boredom are as varied as the feeling itself.

If you want to bring more flow and less boredom to your work-days, these strategies are starting points:

1. **Create challenges.** If your work isn't stimulating, find ways to enrich it with new elements of complexity and challenge. Some people entertain themselves by creating games as they pursue repetitive tasks. One study reported that long-distance truck drivers who played mental games, like counting passing objects, were less bored and also safer drivers.

2. **Interact with other people.** Particularly for extroverts, isolation can feel boring. Look for opportunities to connect, and take time to focus on others around you. For example, Csikszentmihalyi suggests that a supermarket clerk might stimulate flow and also improve service by striking up genuine conversations with customers. You can make tasks more interesting by involving other people or focusing on anyone who might be impacted by your work.

3. **Change your routines.** Vary your normal patterns. Flow is associated with exploration, and even simple variations can make you feel more alive. Work in different spots or find a new place to have coffee or lunch. Meet a wider range of people by broadening your networking activities.

4. **Be quicker and more efficient.** Make the hours at work go faster by speeding up the dull stuff. Cut the time needed to complete routine chores by creating templates and checklists. Look carefully at your normal way of doing things, and remove needless steps. Stay in touch with technology, and experiment with apps that help you speed things up.

5. **Learn something new.** Research says flow is the state most beneficial to learning and forging new neural connections. It works both ways: if you regularly engage in learning, you are less likely to fall into a state of boredom. Activities

where you actively learn tend to capture your attention and feel more like play.

6. **Look for something interesting.** Turn off that negative, internal voice saying, "This is so boring." Instead of sabotaging yourself with whining, search for the interesting aspects of your work. You'll be happier and more successful if you can locate something that grabs your attention. Shake things up by studying a routine task or process and finding ways to do it faster or better.

7. **Stick with doers.** Boredom can be contagious, and if you often spend time with passive, disengaged people, you may start to feel the same way. Look for opportunities to interact with people who are excited by what they do.

8. **Take breaks and move around.** We've talked about the importance of varying the pattern of your workdays and regularly building breaks into your schedule. It's healthy to get up from your desk often and move a little. And be serious about creating a workout routine because physically active people are less likely to become bored.

9. **Develop mindfulness.** By definition, when you're feeling mindful, you're engaged in the moment and aren't bored. A few minutes of deep breathing might help you shake your restlessness and refocus on your goals. A regular mindfulness routine will build your capacity to remain engaged throughout the day.

— KEY TAKEAWAY —

Feeling bored at work is a joy killer, but don't wait around for somebody else to make things better. Life becomes more interesting when you take responsibility for fighting boredom.

Chapter 45

Break Up the Tedium with Memorable Moments

Don't you hate when you look back at the last year, and it seems like week after week was just the same old stuff? Even a comfortable, useful job can feel boring if it seems nobody notices your good work and nothing new ever happens.

Sometimes, though, there may be a perception gap, like when successful work feels flat because nobody recognizes your achievements. Surveys show leaders believe they frequently thank or praise people, yet their team members say they feel unnoticed and undervalued. One reason for this disconnect is the human tendency to focus more on negative feedback and forget about the positive.

Another factor is that if recognition comes along regularly, but always in the same way, we cease to notice it. If your boss says "good job" after every project, the words will mean less over time. For that reason, insightful leaders create celebrations—like new ways of delivering praise, unexpected events, or surprise gifts—to underscore their gratitude and make their praise memorable.

In *The Power of Moments*, authors Chip Heath and Dan Heath explore why unexpected gestures can have an extraordinary impact. *Their research suggests people tend to remember the high and low moments of an experience, and perhaps they recall the beginning and end, but they forget the rest.*

People may find it comfortable when they're in a rut, but they feel more alive when something unusual is happening, the

Heath brothers say. Moments that feel out of the ordinary tend to shape how we judge an experience because those memories are the ones we revisit.

To make a good day on the job feel even better, the Heaths suggest you create a "defining moment"—a short experience that is both meaningful and memorable. Here are ways to reinforce good news and create defining career moments:

1. **Show appreciation.** Complimenting or thanking someone makes both of you feel good. You can make a "thank you" really count by doing something delightful and surprising, like offering food, hanging decorations, wearing a personalized T-shirt, or doing anything likely to cause a person to take a selfie.

2. **Make it social.** A good way to make moments more vivid is to share them with others. Think about how social events like weddings or parties stand out when you recall them years later. You're more likely to remember a work victory if you invite friends or colleagues to celebrate.

3. **Show off your work.** *Doing* a good job feels good. But sometimes your pride intensifies when another person *sees* what you did. If your work is going particularly well, don't assume that others are in a position to observe what you've done. You don't have to brag, but do find a humble, factual way to report on your success.

4. **Create more milestones.** You'll feel more successful if you break your big goals into a series of smaller ones and then enjoy each little victory. Commemorate other important events as well, like your employment anniversary or the acceptance of an award.

5. **Write about it.** Sometimes you don't recognize how great success feels until you describe it in writing. Keeping a record of your achievements and journaling about your successes are good ways to find more joy in your achievements.

6. **All's well that ends well.** When you assess how you spent your hours, you don't remember every little event. The way each day ends tends to skew your recollection of how everything went. So an evening ritual like listing "three good things" can help you wrap up and later recall each day in a more positive way.

— KEY TAKEAWAY —

Even a good job isn't much fun if every day feels the same. Work will be more interesting if you regularly find ways to vary your patterns and do what it takes to make some achievements and events feel special.

Chapter 46

Transparency
Can Lead to Trust

Sometimes workers make themselves needlessly unhappy by waging a futile battle against a boss who wants to keep an eye on all ongoing projects.

I'm thinking of Fred, who mostly enjoyed his job drafting contracts and negotiating small deals for a utility company. His supervisor was my client Diego, and I spoke with Fred while gathering insights from Diego's team.

The two men had joined the company at around the same time, soon after each finished law school. They worked well together on several projects and became good friends. When Diego first became Fred's boss it seemed their friendship would continue smoothly, but when I spoke with Fred, they weren't getting along.

The problems began after Fred moved further away and he requested to telework most days. Diego's boss, Nancy, was not a fan of remote work, but Diego eventually convinced her to require Fred to come to the office only once a week. When Diego proposed the arrangement, he promised Nancy to follow Fred's work carefully and keep her informed about his projects.

Once Fred started working from home, Diego quickly realized that in the past he'd stayed in touch with Fred's activities largely through their frequent informal brainstorming sessions and almost daily morning chats over coffee. They had created no tracking system, and Fred was slow to add his projects into the legal department's filing system.

While Nancy seldom asked Diego for detailed activity reports, now she wanted frequent updates about Fred. To reassure Nancy, Diego started asking Fred for numerous status updates and urged Fred to use digital tracking tools, including a shared project management system.

When I spoke to Fred, he thought his old friend had transformed into a micromanaging monster. The more Diego pushed, the more defensive Fred became. He said, "My work is *my* work, and I'm not sharing drafts."

This scene is playing out in many organizations still learning to manage remote work. Often conscientious professionals like Fred discover that providing abundant information is the secret to earning trust and obtaining more autonomy.

Many busy leaders like Nancy don't have time to micromanage, and they don't want to. Their job is to deliver results, and they feel a need to maintain control. ***Often with a reliable colleague like Fred, it's not that they want to see the details so much as they need to know how to quickly get them, just in case.*** In the old days, if a question arose while Fred was out, colleagues could find the answer on his desk.

As it happened, Diego took a vacation, giving both men a chance to cool down. When they took a fresh look at the situation, Fred acknowledged that he was feeling lonely and out of the loop. He missed their wide-ranging brainstorming sessions and frequent coffee chats. He also was hurt that instead of real conversation Diego seemed interested only in task lists.

Diego said he also missed their discussions, but he was being pressed to show that action steps were well managed. So the two of them collaborated on new communication parameters. Now Fred has mastered the digital tools that allow transparency, and Diego schedules Zoom time for plenty of in-depth discussion.

TRANSPARENCY HAS TRANSFORMED WORK
AND IS CHANGING THE WORLD

Transparency is quickly reshaping the workplace, with new information systems allowing organizations to track every detail, from the supply chain to employment practices.

The good news is that accurate, accessible information not only makes it possible to hold people accountable but also supports a sense of trust. Everybody involved in a process can see the facts, and there's no place to hide incompetency or corruption.

In *Transparency Wave*, successful wealth manager Paul Pagnato* argues that sophisticated new technologies will make it possible for hyper-connected institutions to promote well-being and prosperity for ordinary people.

Pagnato says that in one sense transparency is an attitude. It involves "being vulnerable, open, authentic and real." He argues that successful organizations are now adopting a commitment to absolute transparency, which allows them to pursue innovation at a mind-boggling rate and leave the competition behind. And he says the wave of transparency is unstoppable.

I admit I find aspects of total transparency to be frightening. People do yearn for connection, but we also want privacy and some independence from major institutions. And yet I agree with Pagnato that as professionals and leaders we are wise to adopt transparent practices.

Here are ways transparency can make a difference for workers and organizations:

1. **Good information means successful projects.** A common source of on-the-job stress is the pressure to make decisions without the necessary data. Whether you're manufacturing a product or marketing a service, having accurate, timely info can improve your performance.

2. **Transparency promotes trust.** When nothing can be hidden, there's no reason to be intrusive or suspicious. People get along better when everybody understands what's going on.

3. **Transparency allows alignment of values.** The best places to work are shaped by their core values. When everything from financial results to performance metrics is easy to see, you know whether an organization is upholding its standards and how your work fits into the big picture.

4. **Transparency promotes innovation.** With open and honest discussion, problems are discovered more quickly, and people can more easily work together to find solutions.

5. **Transparency makes it easy to outsource.** As you progress in your career, a key to success is getting somebody else to do the things you dislike, don't have time for, or aren't good at. Delegating low-value activities allows you to maximize the return on your time and resources. Pagnato's advice is "whenever possible, outsource."

— KEY TAKEAWAY —

The age of transparency is here. You will enhance your performance when you recognize that sharing accurate, timely information can speed the process, improve results, and lead to trusting relationships.

Chapter 47

Physical Space Can Promote Happiness and Productivity

For almost a century scientists have been telling organizations that the space where people work impacts their success. Research says the physical environment where you complete your tasks influences both your creativity and your ability to solve complicated problems. Studies show that a room's temperature, lighting, ceiling height, air quality, and noise level all might influence the quality of your work, mood, and health.

In recent years attention has focused on finding workstation configurations that promote collaboration and innovation. Now designers are exploring better ways to avoid gathering workers too close together for good health.

As employers redefine their idea of "the office," some innovative companies have followed the example of universities, where students work in many settings, from dorm rooms to libraries to communal gathering points. The campuses of tech giants Google and Apple provide staffers with a choice of workspaces, from restorative outdoor areas to vast rooms designed to generate energy and excitement.

Whether they are at home or in corporate headquarters, many people work in spaces that are less than ideal. For them, the question is how to make the best of a situation not designed to support their best work.

It's possible to enhance your work area. By considering the design elements that influence your mood and how you work, you may spot easy-to-do improvements. Here are strategies for creating a more satisfying workspace:

1. **Connect with the outdoors.** People are born with an affinity to the natural world, and access to green space can make us healthier and happier. The ideal arrangement is to have a window nearby, preferably one with a view of nature. Even if you work in a windowless room, green plants, art work, or other reminders of natural beauty may help you feel and work better.

2. **Make your space reflect your values.** Even if your spot is just the designated section of a table, it says something about you. If it looks tidy and organized, colleagues may assume you have things under control. If you want to be seen as creative, personalize your space with small pieces of art, a lamp, or elegant pens and other tools.

3. **Ergonomics matter.** When you start a new work setup, take the time to do an ergonomic assessment. Protect yourself from neck and back pain or sore wrists and fingers. Consider factors like your chair height, equipment spacing, and your typical desk posture.

4. **Experiment.** Your work setup doesn't have to remain frozen in place for the duration of your time there. Occasionally freshening things up can be energizing. Pause to notice how things look, how your space makes you feel, and whether your tools and arrangements function as well as they might.

5. **Color.** In her popular book *Joyful*, designer Ingrid Fetell Lee explores how our physical surroundings impact our moods. Drawing on neuroscience, she says one setting may make you feel anxious or competitive while another makes you want to share. Because people work better in bright rooms, she suggests using color and lightening surfaces to create a sense of light.

6. **Tidy up.** For many people, working in an orderly environment feels good, giving you a more positive outlook and allowing ideas and inspiration to flow. In *Joy at Work*, Marie Kondo says if you look after things that make your work possible, both your attitude and your behavior toward others change, leading you to better results.

— KEY TAKEAWAY —

The space where you work can impact your performance and well-being. Whether it means redecorating an office or rearranging the space where you set up your laptop, a workplace makeover can bring you fresh energy.

Chapter 48

Manage Money to Create Career Flexibility

Too often I hear from people who are unhappy at work and resent their employers, mostly because they feel trapped. They dream of a new job or maybe a different occupation, but their finances won't allow them to shift. Some professionals are caught by "golden handcuffs," meaning they're paid too well to allow them to easily leave.

We enjoy our jobs more when it feels like we're there by choice, and financial flexibility can give us a sense of freedom. Journalist, author, and financial expert Kerry Hannon* says, "When you're financially fit, you have options about the life you live and the work you do—whether it's for pay or pro bono, full-time or part-time."

Here are ten of Kerry's favorite tips for managing your money and becoming financially nimble:

1. **Do a budget.** No eye-rolling. Each January, make this a habit. Start by writing down your recurring fixed expenses, such as your mortgage or rent payment, health insurance premiums, utilities, and so forth. Last year's outlays can provide a guide. Where can you get lean? Are there expenditures from last year that you can trim back this year?

   Pencil in discretionary expenses that you expect, but don't know exact amounts for—like groceries and restaurants and entertainment. Prepare for unavoidable costs such as unexpected medical bills or home repairs. Make note of any fun events in the offing, like weddings or travel that will bring related bills. Do your best to take a crack at what this spending might add up to, and tuck them into your budget.

2. **Review your credit report.** The three big credit bureaus—Experian, TransUnion and Equifax—provide everyone with one free credit report annually; it's the law. Request one at *AnnualCreditReport.com*. When you get it, look for possible errors. Even if your name is misspelled or your Social Security number is incorrect, that can hurt your ability to get a credit card or loan. If you find a mistake, contact the credit bureau or bureaus where you discovered the error and explain the error in writing. And write to the company that provided information to the credit bureau.

3. **Set aside regular "money dates" with your spouse or partner, if you have one.** Unromantic? Perhaps, but hear me out. I advise setting regular money conversation dates where you can talk about your finances as a team: your dreams, goals, and fears. Remind each other that love and respect come down to honesty and financial openness.

4. **Pay it down.** If possible, pay off outstanding high-interest credit card debts, college loans, and auto loans. Or at the very least take a good whack at right sizing. This can take some time, but there's nothing as energizing as a clean balance sheet. *One of my favorite cautionary lines: debt is a dream killer.*

5. **Save, save, save.** It's smart to have a cushion of six months or more of living expenses, in cash or cash-equivalent funds, set aside for unexpected emergencies. This is especially true if you're planning to make a transition, whether to a new field of work or to follow a dream.

6. **Lower your housing costs.** For more freedom from financial pressure, it might make sense to move to a smaller

home or even relocate to a cheaper area. You may have to take a salary cut if you change jobs, so it might make sense to look for work in an area where the cost of living is lower.

7. **Refinance your mortgage.** Moving is kind of drastic for most of us. Refinancing is the easier option. The goal is to lock in a fixed rate and cut your mortgage interest by at least 1 percent. That way, you'll likely break even on refinancing costs within two years. Figure out how much you can save over time with an online refinancing calculator.

8. **Boost your credit score.** Your eyes glaze over at the very sound of it. Mine do, too. But that nebulous three-digit number is one figure you absolutely can't ignore today. It impacts your entire financial life. Here's why: If you need to borrow funds to start a business, lenders use it to determine whether they should lend you money and what your interest rate will be. Landlords may use it when deciding whether to rent to you. *And if you're switching to a new company, many employers review it when deciding whether to hire you.* The most obvious way to keep your score in shape . . . pay your bills on time.

9. **Get physically fit.** When you're in good shape physically, you have the energy, positivity, and can-do spirit that come from fitness. And it can go a long way to helping stave off medical bills.

10. **Ramp up your financial mojo.** It's important to have an overall financial plan, including an estate plan, and to rebalance your investments periodically to reflect your risk tolerance. You might start with hiring a financial adviser, if you don't already have one on your team, to help answer your questions and lend a sharp eye to your total financial picture. For unbiased guidance, look for a fee-only planner with the Certified Financial Planner designation. Also consider starting a money book club or a money-circle

discussion group. It will encourage you to read useful books and have regular conversations about finances.

— KEY TAKEAWAY —

You can't have career flexibility without financial stability. If you take control of your finances now and start gradually building your savings, you will lay groundwork for freedom in the future. It's easier to love your job when you know you have the power to leave.

For more tips, see Kerry's website:
www.kerryhannon.com.

Chapter 49

Time to Redesign Your Job? Or Add a Side Gig?

I often talk about "your job" as though I assume you have a single position of employment. But that's mostly for simplicity. The fact is that job structures vary widely. What you regard as your "job" might include various employers, clients, tasks, skills, and activities.

Earlier, I shared a simplified mind map of my career encompassing multiple contracts and several types of freelance activity—both paid and unpaid—that I regard as part of my "job." My collection of work looks less like a traditional job and more like what lawyers call "a bundle of sticks." In other words, it's an untidy mix of relationships and situations that somehow are happily tied together.

Even if you work for one employer and have a fixed position description, it's wise to think of your job as a bundle of current tasks and future possibilities. That's because nothing ever stays the same. Either your job is growing and changing to keep up with the times, or it'll face challenges in the future.

Highly successful people tend to be entrepreneurial, which means they don't assume the status quo will continue. Wherever they may be, they constantly think of future possibilities and look for ways to add more value.

These days there's not much job security, but there is plenty of opportunity for folks who keep looking ahead, learning, and hustling. In this chapter I discuss three ways people are continuing to expand and reinvent their jobs and are finding ways to create their own growth, happiness, and security.

RECRAFT YOUR PRIMARY JOB

Savvy professionals seldom work their way slowly up a ladder. Instead, they find ways to produce beyond their job descriptions, gradually expanding their responsibilities and making their work more interesting.

Job crafting is a term used when workers redesign their jobs to better match their strengths and interests. Job crafting might involve changing functions, tasks, and relationships to make your position feel like a better fit.

While some managers work with staffers to make their roles more engaging, many workers don't expect that to happen. They gradually make the changes on their own and eventually get recognition for their broader slate of activities.

If you want to make your work more meaningful by job crafting, try these steps:

1. **Find efficiencies.** You have the best view of how your current tasks might be performed more efficiently. Look for ways to delete wasted steps and improve your processes. Delegate, renegotiate, or say "no" to activities that don't serve a purpose. Fulfill your responsibilities increasingly well, as you begin to add value in new ways.

2. **Identify goals and interests.** Determine what you do well and enjoy. Consider how to apply your skills to useful activities that would be more interesting. Develop a vision of the kind of job you want next.

3. **Understand what your employer needs.** Study the vision, strategy, and current challenges faced by your organization. Understand what your bosses need and want.

4. **Match your strengths to their needs.** Once you understand where you want to go, look for ways to use your relevant skills to support your employer's strategies. Volunteer to take on tasks that will allow you to grow at the same time you're helping team success.

5. **Act as if.** Once your bigger, better job is in sight, act as if you already have it. Instead of waiting for a promotion, perform new high-value tasks and make sure your supervisor is happy about what you're doing. Eventually, ask for a position description that includes all your great work.

TAKE ON A SECOND JOB

Surveys vary, but some say that half of American workers have at least an occasional second job. The percentage of younger people with side gigs is even higher.

An obvious reason for this huge trend is that many people need a secondary income to feed their families. Others want the security of another financial stream. But the situation is more complex than that.

Many people launch a side hustle—even if they enjoy their day job—because they want to turn their hobby into a business. Others are eager to pursue a passion project.

In a podcast, Austin Belcak* described how he loves working as a Microsoft director of partner development. But what brought him public attention is his side gig as a job search expert. Through his firm, Cultivated Culture, Austin helps recent college graduates earn job offers from leading tech companies.

Austin has come a long way since finishing college in 2013, without tech connections or experience. To make the leap to a top company, he researched every aspect of corporate recruiting. Then he went through the process himself, snagging multiple offers.

Because he knew how it felt to be overwhelmed by the job market, Austin created his side business to share what he'd learned. At first he wasn't sure Microsoft would approve, but when his bosses heard about what he was doing, they applauded his work.

A side hustle can change your life. In addition to helping you feel financially secure, it provides a path for developing new skills, broadening your network, and building your confidence.

BUILD A PORTFOLIO CAREER

A side hustle usually means a second way to earn money, in addition to your main job. *But some people pull together a mixed collection of occupations and projects, none of which looks like a primary job.*

Karen Deans, who created the illustrations in this book, is an artist and designer. Her website, *karendeans.com*, shows some of her work, ranging from colorful posters to clever postcards, magazine covers, and book illustrations.

Karen is also a writer. She has a variety of commercial contracts. She writes children's books, like the charming *Swing Sisters*, which tells the true story of African American orphans in segregated Mississippi who traveled the globe as an all-girl swing band.

Once, multitalented Karen struggled to pick one career path, trying to decide whether to be an artist, a writer, or maybe a full-time mom. Now, Karen says, she wakes up early every morning, excited to plunge into a packed workday. Some of her joy and energy come from knowing she doesn't *have* to choose just one job.

If you're thinking of forging a portfolio of work, start by creating a good system for organizing your schedule and keeping track of your projects. If you're launching a business, become familiar with the basics like bookkeeping. Look for anchor clients. Also, keep building your network, both in person and online.

— KEY TAKEAWAY —

When your job is not satisfying, there are many ways to change things up. You can take steps to expand and modify your current position. Or you can bring more excitement and security into your work life by creating side gigs. One day you might want to pull together a mixed portfolio of jobs and businesses.

Chapter 50

Ten Key Takeaways for Finding Your Happy at Work

In this last chapter we focus on the future—your future.

Here are ten reminders to help you continue to create joy, meaning, and success in your work.

1. **You can grow.** You have tremendous power to change, develop, and create a work life and long-term career filled with joy, meaning, and success. Humans are learning machines, and you are well equipped to increase your skills, expertise, and even intelligence; to develop more confidence, grit, and resilience; and to become more like the person you want to be.

2. **Work can feel more like play.** Sometimes the difference between work and play is your attitude. Both are more satisfying if you approach them with a positive mindset and considerable effort. Both work and play are more fun when you invest concentration, skill, commitment, and learning.

3. **Care for yourself.** It's difficult to thrive at work if you're exhausted, unhealthy, or trapped in negativity. Doing your best work—and enjoying what you do—starts with cultivating well-being and caring for your physical, emotional, mental, and spiritual fitness. These four realms of body, mind, spirit, and heart are so tightly connected that when you take better care of any one of the four, your whole life might benefit.

4. **Focus on purpose, people, and performance.** When you are bogged down at work, when you don't know what to do, think about the three *P*s of the Engagement Triangle. Get moving by taking small action steps that reflect your purpose and values, positively impact other people, and support the kind of performance that meets your standards and gets the job done well.

5. **Tiny steps can take you far.** You can accomplish big things and create sweeping change if you commit yourself to moving forward "one sugar grain at a time." The secret is establishing a pace of tiny actions and sticking with it. Your process will be more powerful if you step back and look at the big picture, identify a long-term vision, create a series of specific goals, and track your sugar grains of activity.

6. **Success follows happiness.** You don't have to choose between a meaningful, happy life and a successful career. You're more likely to succeed at your job if you have a positive attitude and feel happy. Positivity helps you spot opportunities, stay motivated, remain healthy, and get along with other people.

7. **Choose positivity.** You *can* become more optimistic and upbeat, even if times are hard and you were born a pessimist. One useful technique is to reject the negative voice in your head and replace repetitive internal comments with more optimistic language. Among other ways to cultivate positivity are being kind to someone, summoning up a feeling of gratitude, enjoying a small success, journaling, or taking a walk outdoors.

8. **Relationships matter.** Humans are hardwired to need connection with other humans. To be well and perform at your best, you need relationships with other people. Building your network of relationships is critical to your happiness and the success of your career. A large, diverse network

will help you find opportunities, build resilience, and keep learning.

9. **Change your habits to boost performance.** Much of your life is shaped by learned routines you follow mindlessly. Your automatic habits save time and limit the pressure of making decisions, but some keep you stuck in patterns that aren't fulfilling or effective. By tweaking old habits and consciously building new ones, you can gradually reshape your work life.

10. **Meditate.** When you are mindful, you're consciously paying attention to what's happening now, you're in the moment, and you're not bored or judgmental. By practicing mindfulness exercises, you can reduce stress, support stronger social relationships, better control your emotions, lower your blood pressure, spark creativity, and enhance your ability to pay attention and make decisions.

I am grateful to you for reading this book, and I wish you a meaningful and happy life.

APPENDIX: *JAZZED ABOUT WORK* PODCAST GUESTS AND EPISODES

Jazzed About Work, a podcast hosted by author Beverly Jones, focuses on finding joy, meaning, and success in your career. It is produced by WOUB Public Media at Ohio University in Athens, Ohio. Among other podcast sites, episodes are archived at:

- NPR.org, at *www.npr.org*
- WOUB.org, at *www.woub.org*
- Apple Podcasts, at *podcasts.apple.com*

Following are the *Jazzed About Work* guests mentioned in this book, along with topics and dates when their episodes were released:

- **Shawn Askinosie,** February 13, 2020, Seek meaningful work as you consider your whole life
- **Carla Bass,** January 2, 2020, Powerful writing empowers your success
- **Austin Belcak,** February 15, 2018, Unconventional job search strategies
- **Kerry Hannon:**
  - April 27, 2017, Tips for making the best of your current job
  - September 13, 2018, Tips for making career shifts
  - August 29, 2019, You're not too old to open a business
  - August 27, 2020, How to find a remote job and thrive
- **Tom Hodson,** who serves as a guest host and interviews Bev Jones as the expert:
  - January 24, 2018, Navigating a transition in your work life
  - May 24, 2018, Staying engaged in work
  - October 11, 2018, How to beat the career blahs
  - April 11, 2019, Branding and your career
  - May 1, 2019, Moving from career to retirement
  - July 18, 2019, Moving past career failures
  - November 7, 2019, Is networking creepy or critical?

- March 12, 2020, Entrepreneurship tips for potential retirees
- March 26, 2020, Tips for planning your entrepreneurial career
- **Rob Jones,** August 1, 2019, Diversity programs are dated and need reinvention
- **Susan P. Joyce,** January 3, 2019, Expert LinkedIn tips
- **Dayna Bowen Matthew,** July 20, 2017, Equity expert discusses racial inequality
- **Mark Miller,** January 17, 2019, Growth through trauma
- **Paul Pagnato,** April 21, 2020, Transparency changes everything
- **Klaus Peters,** February 28, 2018, Treating everybody like somebody
- **Dan Schawbel,** October 22, 2018, Job expert advises communicating in person
- **Bob Shaff,** August 15, 2019, Even shy people can be great connectors
- **Maura Nevel Thomas,** December 19, 2019, Manage your attention
- **Gayle Williams-Byers:**
  - May 25, 2017, Challenges of a judicial career
  - January 31, 2019, Tips for promoting well-being
- **"Zapponians" Derrin Hawkins, Kelly Smith, and Tia Zuniga:**
  - April 9, 2020, How Zappos employees crowdsourced writing a book on the company's core values

BIBLIOGRAPHY

Achor, Shawn. *Big Potential: How Transforming the Pursuit of Success Raises Our Achievement, Happiness, and Well-Being.* New York: Random House, 2018.

————. *The Happiness Advantage: How a Positive Brain Fuels Success in Work and Life.* New York: Currency, 2018.

Amabile, Teresa, and Steve Kramer. "Small Wins and Feeling Good." *Harvard Business Review*, May 13, 2011. *hbr.org*.

Askinosie, Shawn. *Meaningful Work: A Quest to Do Great Business, Find Your Calling, and Feed Your Soul.* New York: Penguin Publishing Group, 2017.

Bass, Carla D. *Write to Influence! Personnel Appraisals, Resumes, Awards, Grants, Scholarships, Internships, Reports, Bid Proposals, Web Pages, Marketing, and More.* Marshall, VA: Orlean Press, 2019.

Bavishi, Avni, Martin D. Slade, and Becca R. Levy. "A Chapter a Day: Association of Book Reading with Longevity." *Social Science & Medicine*. US National Library of Medicine, September 2016. *www.ncbi.nlm.nih.gov*.

Begley, Sharon. *Train Your Mind, Change Your Brain: How a New Science Reveals Our Extraordinary Potential to Transform Ourselves.* New York: Ballantine Books, 2008.

Belitz, Charlene, and Meg Lundstrom. *The Power of Flow.* New York: Random House, 1998.

Benson, Herbert, and William Proctor. *Beyond the Relaxation Response: How to Harness the Healing Power of Your Personal Beliefs.* New York: Times Books, 1984.

————. *The Breakout Principle: How to Activate the Natural Trigger that Maximizes Creativity, Athletic Performance, Productivity, and Personal Well-Being.* New York: Scribner, 2003.

Buettner, Dan. *The Blue Zones: Lessons for Living Longer from the People Who've Lived the Longest.* Washington, DC: National Geographic, 2008.

————. *The Blue Zones of Happiness: Lessons from the World's Happiest People.* Washington, DC: National Geographic, 2019.

Buzan, Tony, and Barry Buzan. *The Mind Map Book: How to Use Radiant Thinking to Maximize Your Brain's Untapped Potential.* New York: Plume, 1993.

Cacioppo, John T., and William Patrick. *Loneliness: Human Nature and the Need for Social Connection.* New York: W. W. Norton and Company, 2009.

Carnegie, Dale. *How to Win Friends & Influence People.* New York: Pocket Books, 1998.

Chaleff, Ira. *The Courageous Follower: Standing Up to and for Our Leaders.* San Francisco: Berrett-Koehler Publishers, 1995.

Chopra, Deepak, and Rudolph E. Tanzi. *Super Brain: Unleashing the Explosive Power of Your Mind to Maximize Health, Happiness, and Spiritual Well-Being.* New York: Harmony Books, 2012.

Christakis, Nicholas A., and James H. Fowler. "When You Smile, the World Smiles with You." In *Connected: The Amazing Power of Social Networks and How They Shape Our Lives.* New York: Bay Back Books, 2011.

Clear, James. *Atomic Habits: Tiny Changes, Remarkable Results: An Easy & Proven Way to Build Good Habits & Break Bad Ones.* New York: Avery, 2018.

Colvin, Geoff. *Talent Is Overrated: What Really Separates World-Class Performers from Everybody Else.* New York: Portfolio, 2008.

Coyle, Daniel. *The Culture Code: The Secrets of Highly Successful Groups.* London: Bantam Books, 2018.

Csikszentmihalyi, Mihaly. *Flow: The Psychology of Optimal Experience.* New York: Harper Row, 2009.

Dagostino, Mark. *The Power of WOW: How to Electrify Your Work and Your Life by Putting Service First.* Dallas, TX: BenBella Books, Inc., 2019.

Davidson, Richard J., and Sharon Begley. *The Emotional Life of Your Brain: How Its Unique Patterns Affect the Way You Think, Feel, and Live—and How You Can Change Them.* New York: Hudson Street Press, 2012.

Dean, Jeremy. *Making Habits, Breaking Habits: Why We Do Things, Why We Don't, and How to Make Any Change Stick.* Richmond, VA: Oneworld, 2013.

Deans, Karen. *Swing Sisters: The Story of the International Sweethearts of Rhythm.* New York: Holiday House, 2015.

Denworth, Lydia. *Friendship: The Evolution, Biology, and Extraordinary Power of Life's Fundamental Bond.* New York: W. W. Norton, 2020.

DeSteno, David. "Why Gratitude Is Wasted on Thanksgiving." *New York Times,* November 23, 2019, Sunday Review, *nytimes.com.*

Duckworth, Angela. *Grit: The Power of Passion and Perseverance.* New York: Scribner, 2016.

Duhigg, Charles. *The Power of Habit: Why We Do What We Do in Life and Business.* New York: Random House, 2012.

Dweck, Carol S. *Mindset: The New Psychology of Success.* New York: Ballantine Books, 2008.

Emmons, Robert. "Why Gratitude Is Good." *Greater Good Magazine,* November 16, 2010. *greatergood.berkeley.edu.*

Fredrickson, Barbara. *Positivity: Groundbreaking Research to Release Your Inner Optimist and Thrive.* Richmond, VA: Oneworld, 2010.

Friedman, Ronald M. "The Power of Place." In *The Best Place to Work: The Art and Science of Creating an Extraordinary Workplace.* New York: Penguin Putnam Inc., 2016.

Gallwey, W. Timothy. *The Inner Game of Stress: Outsmart Life's Challenges and Fulfill Your Potential.* New York: Random House, 2009.

———. *The Inner Game of Tennis.* New York: Random House, 1974.

———. *The Inner Game of Work.* New York: Random House, 1999.

Gladwell, Malcolm. *Outliers: The Story of Success.* New York: Back Bay Books/Little, Brown, 2008.

Goleman, Daniel. *Altered Traits.* New York: Penguin Group, 2018.

———. *The Brain and Emotional Intelligence: New Insights.* Northampton, MA: More Than Sound, 2011.

———. *Emotional Intelligence.* New York: Bantam Books, 1995.

———. *Focus: The Hidden Driver of Excellence.* New York: HarperCollins, 2013.

———. "Part I." In *Focus: The Hidden Driver of Excellence.* London: Bloomsbury, 2013.

———. *Social Intelligence: The New Science of Human Relationships.* New York: Bantam Books, 2007.

Grant, Adam M. *Give and Take: A Revolutionary Approach to Success.* New York: Viking, 2013.

Haden, Jeff. *The Motivation Myth: How High Achievers Really Set Themselves Up to Win.* New York: Portfolio, 2018.

Hannon, Kerry. *Great Pajama Jobs: Your Complete Guide to Working from Home.* Hoboken, NJ: Wiley, 2020.

———. *Love Your Job: The New Rules of Career Happiness.* Hoboken, NJ: Wiley, 2015.

———. *Never Too Old to Get Rich: The Entrepreneur's Guide to Starting a Business Mid-Life.* Hoboken, NJ: Wiley, 2019.

———. *What's Next? Follow Your Passion and Find Your Dream Job.* San Francisco: Chronicle Books, 2010.

Harder, David. *The Workplace Engagement Solution: Find a Common Mission, Vision, and Purpose with All of Today's Employees.* Wayne, NJ: Career Press, 2017.

Harris, Russ. *The Confidence Gap.* Boulder, CO: Trumpeter Boulder, 2011.

Heath, Chip, and Dan Heath. *The Power of Moments: Why Certain Experiences Have Extraordinary Impact.* New York: Simon & Schuster, 2017.

Holiday, Ryan. *The Obstacle Is the Way: The Timeless Art of Turning Trials into Triumph.* New York: Portfolio/Penguin, 2014.

Horstman, Judith. *The Scientific American Healthy Aging Brain: The Neuroscience of Making the Most of Your Mature Mind.* San Francisco: Jossey-Bass, 2012.

Iacoboni, Marco. *Mirroring People: The New Science of How We Connect with Others.* New York: Farrar, Straus, and Giroux, 2008.

Isaacson, Walter. *Benjamin Franklin: An American Life,* 1–101. New York: Simon & Schuster, 2006.

Jones, Beverly E. *Jazzed About Work.* WOUB Public Media. WOUB Public Media, April 18, 2017. *woub.org.*

———. *Think Like an Entrepreneur, Act Like a CEO: 50 Indispensable Tips to Help You Stay Afloat, Bounce Back, and Get Ahead at Work.* Wayne, NJ: Career Press, 2015.

Kabat-Zinn, Jon. *Wherever You Go, There You Are.* London: Piatkus, 2004.

Kay, Katty, and Claire Shipman. *The Confidence Code: The Science and Art of Self-Assurance—What Women Should Know.* New York: HarperBusiness, 2014.

Kondo, Marie, and Scott Sonenshein. *Joy at Work: Organizing Your Professional Life.* New York: Little, Brown, 2020.

Langer, Ellen J. *Counter Clockwise: Mindful Health and the Power of Possibility.* New York: Ballantine Books, 2009.

———. *Mindfulness.* Cambridge, MA: Lifelong Books/Da Capo Press, 2010.

———. "The Myth of Delayed Gratification." In *The Power of Mindful Learning,* 51–66. Boston: Da Capo Press, 1997.

Lee, Ingrid Fetell. "Energy." In *Joyful: The Surprising Power of Ordinary Things to Create Extraordinary Happiness.* New York: Little, Brown, 2020.

Leonard, George. *Mastery: The Keys to Success and Long-Term Fulfillment.* New York: Dutton, 1991.

Loehr, Jim, and Tony Schwartz. *The Power of Full Engagement: Managing Energy, Not Time, Is the Key to High Performance and Personal Renewal.* New York: Free Press, 2005.

Lorenzo, Rocio, Nicole Voigt, Miki Tsusaka, Matt Krentz, and Katie Abouzahr. "How Diverse Leadership Teams Boost Innovation." Boston Consulting Group, January 23, 2013. *www.bcg.com.*

Mariotti, Steve. *Goodbye Homeboy.* Dallas, TX: BenBella Books, 2019.

Matthew, Dayna Bowen. *Just Medicine: A Cure for Racial Inequality in American Health Care.* New York: New York University Press, 2018.

McGonigal, Kelly. "Embrace Life." In *The Joy of Movement: How Exercise Helps Us Find Happiness, Hope, Connection, and Courage,* 153–78. New York: Avery, 2019.

McGraw, Tim. *Grit & Grace: Train the Mind, Train the Body, Own Your Life.* New York: HarperCollins, 2019.

Miller, Mark. *Jolt: Stories of Trauma and Transformation.* New York: Post Hill Press, 2018.

Murthy, Vivek H. *Together:The Healing Power of Human Connection in a Sometimes Lonely World.* New York: HarperCollins, 2020.

Newport, Cal. *Deep Work: Rules for Focused Success in a Distracted World.* New York: Grand Central Publishing, 2016.

Pagnato, Paul. *Transparency Wave.* Reston, VA: Transparency Press, 2020.

Patrick, William, and John T. Cacioppo. *Loneliness: Human Nature and the Need for Social Connection.* New York: W. W. Norton and Company, 2009.

Peters, Klaus. "Do You Remember Earl G Duffy, Hotelier Extraordinaire?" LinkedIn. Accessed April 25, 2020. *www .linkedin.com.*

Price, Beverly Jones. *Report on the Status of Women at Ohio University.* Athens, OH: Ohio University Libraries, 1972.

Rath, Tom, and Jim K. Harter. *Wellbeing: The Five Essential Elements.* New York: Gallup Press, 2014.

Rauch, Jonathan. *The Happiness Curve: Why Life Gets Better After 50.* New York: Thomas Dunne Books/McMillan, 2018.

Reasoner, Harry. "The Reasoner Report, Inner Game of Tennis." YouTube. *The Reasoner Report,* ABC News, May 19, 2012. *www .youtube.com.*

Ruiz, Miguel. "The Second Agreement." In *The Four Agreements: A Practical Guide to Personal Freedom.* San Rafael, CA: Amber-Allen Publishing, 2017.

Schawbel, Dan. *Back to Human: How Great Leaders Create Connection in the Age of Isolation.* New York: Da Capo Press, 2018.

Seligman, Martin E. P. *Authentic Happiness: Using the New Positive Psychology to Realize Your Potential for Lasting Fulfillment.* New York: Free Press, 2002.

———. *Flourish: A Visionary New Understanding of Happiness and Well-Being.* New York: Atria, 2013.

———. *Learned Optimism: How to Change Your Mind and Your Life.* New York: Vintage Books, 2006.

Staats, Bradley R. *Never Stop Learning: Stay Relevant, Reinvent Yourself, and Thrive.* Boston: Harvard Business Review Press, 2018.

Strozzi-Heckler, Richard. *Holding the Center: Sanctuary in a Time of Confusion.* Berkeley, CA: Frog, 1997.

Thomas, Maura Nevel. *Attention Management: How to Create Success and Gain Productivity—Every Day.* Naperville, IL: Simple Truths, 2019.

———. *Work without Walls: An Executive's Guide to Attention Management, Productivity, and the Future of Work.* Austin, TX: Burget Ave. Press, 2017.

Vanderkam, Laura. *Off the Clock: Feel Less Busy while Getting More Done.* New York: Portfolio/Penguin, 2018.

Vernikos, Joan. *Sitting Kills, Moving Heals: How Simple, Everyday Movement Will Prevent Pain, Illness, and Early Death—and Exercise Alone Won't.* Fresno, CA: Quill Driver Books, 2011.

Webb, Caroline. *How to Have a Good Day*. New York: Crown Business, 2016.

Zander, Rosamund Stone, and Benjamin Zander. *The Art of Possibility*. New York: Penguin Books, 2002.

ABOUT THE AUTHOR

Beverly Jones is a master of reinvention. She led university programs for women before trailblazing her career as a Washington lawyer and *Fortune* 500 energy executive. Throughout her varied work life, she has mentored other professionals and leaders to grow and thrive.

Today Jones is a high-profile executive coach and leadership consultant, helping professionals of all ages find joy and meaning in their careers, shift directions, and become more productive. Based in the Washington, DC, area, she works with clients spread across the country, including accomplished leaders in major federal agencies, Congress, universities, and businesses from emerging entrepreneurs to large corporations.

Jones is a popular speaker and facilitator, as well as a visiting executive with Ohio University's Voinovich School of Leadership and Public Affairs. She frequently writes about career management and success, well-being, and thriving at work, including at *Job-Hunt.org*, where she is a networking expert.

Career Press published Jones's first book, *Think Like an Entrepreneur, Act Like a CEO*. Her podcast, *Jazzed About Work*, is produced by WOUB Media and heard on NPR.org. Jones is vice chair of a nonprofit journalism foundation, Foothills Forum. It's located in beautiful Rappahannock County, Virginia, where she and her husband, former *Washington Post* ombudsman Andy Alexander, often work from their farmhouse.

You can follow Jones on Twitter @beverlyejones and on LinkedIn at *www.linkedin.com/in/beverly-jones-coach-author/*.

Her website is *www.clearwaysconsulting.com*.